GNYS AT WRK

GNYS AT WRK,

A Child Learns to Write and Read

Glenda L. Bissex
/ / (

HARVARD UNIVERSITY PRESS
Cambridge, Massachusetts
and London, England

Library of Congress Cataloging in Publication Data

Bissex, Glenda L
  Gnys at wrk.

  Bibliography: p.
  Includes index.
  1. Reading (Primary) 2. Reading readiness.
I. Title.
LB1525.24.B57   372.4   80-14558
ISBN 0-674-35485-0 (cloth)
ISBN 0-674-35490-7 (paper)

Preface

This is an account of one child's learning to read and write, from the beginnings of literacy at age five up to age eleven.

When I began taking notes about my infant son's development, I did not know I was gathering "data" for "research"; I was a mother with a propensity for writing things down. Because of my experience in Courtney Cazden's Child Language course at Harvard, I was particularly interested in my son's language development; and as an English teacher just retrained in reading, I wanted to observe his learning to read. When Paul started spelling, I was amazed and fascinated. Only somewhat later did I learn of Charles Read's research on children's invented spelling. Excited by his work, I started seeing my notes as "data."

During my initial analysis of the first year of Paul's learning to spell and to read, I was looking for ways in which these learnings were related through his understanding of orthographic principles. But the relations I found did not turn out to be as interesting to me as the evidence I saw of flexibility, of changes in learning strategies, during this period. Since a child can only begin to learn printed language from a very incomplete understanding of how it operates, changes in strategy, changes in the concepts about printed language that govern strategy, seem necessary for learning. They reflect the child's expanding grasp of the complex principles of written language.

Later, looking over my observations of six years of Paul's development, I saw other patterns — partly because the longer time perspective allowed them to emerge, and partly because my vision had been enriched by a seminar, The Child as Reader and Writer, given by Patricia Carini and Jessica Howard at the Prospect School. What Paul wrote as well as how he spelled it now became important to the study. The more I looked at the forms and themes and styles of his writing, the more I understood of him as a reader and as a person. In this longer view, the relationship between his reading and writing appeared more personal, residing in meanings as well as skills.

In the process of looking at and trying to organize my material and my thoughts about it, I more than once sought a scheme, a set of categories, a philosophic view — some preexisting form to shape it. Israel Scheffler gave me wise and difficult advice when he observed that categories, by directing our efforts to pigeonholing rather than looking at our material, may make us see less of it, not more. Carol Chomsky, more than once, urged me to make my own maps of the territory I was exploring, which is what, at heart, I wanted to do. So what I have seen here has come mainly from looking again and again at my material in all its details, and trying to find its form while respecting its irregularities. I found in the end that generalizations, as they distill meanings, may also dispel them by abstracting away the very particulars that gave them life.

What I hope this study offers, rather than generalizations to be "applied" to other children, is encouragement to look at individuals in the act of learning. And I do mean *act,* with all that implies of drama and action.

A case study is essentially an attempt to understand another person through enlightened subjectivity, which seeks both to share the experience of another and to reflect upon it from a distance. Parent-researchers may be long on sharing and short on distancing. I have tried to provide enough raw material so that readers can compensate for my lapses through their own analyses. A case study this detailed and extended over time would have been unmanageable were I not a parent.

The other side of the coin—the researcher as parent—has been more neglected, and researchers studying their own children generally have not discussed the personal side of the "scientific" relationship. I have wondered about their experiences and been concerned about my relationship with my son, especially as Paul grew older and more aware of my researching.

At the beginning, Paul was an unconscious subject, unaware of the significance of my tape recorder and notebook. When he first became aware, at about age six, he was pleased by my interest and attention. By seven, he had become an observer of his own progress. When I worked on my initial analysis of the first year's data (5:1-6:1) and had Paul's early writings spread out on my desk, he loved to look at them with me and try to read them. They offered the challenge of breaking what then appeared to him a code, and their visible evidence of his progress since he had written them gave him a sense of achievement. "I notice I didn't know about silent *e*'s then," he once observed (7:8), referring to such spellings as HAT (hate) and LIK (like). About this same time Paul had observed me writing down a question he had asked about spelling, and I inquired how he felt about my writing it down. "Then I know that when I'm older I can see the stuff I asked when I was little," he commented.

At eight he was self-conscious enough to object to obvious observation and note taking, which I then stopped. One day when I was making informal observations of his laterality, he looked at my notebook to see what I was jotting down and said, "I don't like to be charted on everything I do" (8:0). Paul still brought his writings (except personal ones) to me, sharing my sense of their importance. At nine he became a participant in the research, interested in thinking about *why* he had written or read things as he once had. When I speculated aloud that his early oral reading had been aimed at receiving adult feedback and correction, he argued instead that *he* needed to hear the words in order to know if they were right.

The study has become a special bond between us, an interest

we share in each other's work, a mutual enjoyment of Paul's early childhood and of his growing up. I have come to appreciate certain qualities in my son that I might not have seen except through the eyes of this study.

Since Paul became a fluent writer (using his own spelling system) before he became a fluent reader, I have described his development in writing first and then his growth in reading. The processes seem separable though only in some ways separate. Later chapters of this study will attempt to restore their naturally closer relationship as aspects of literacy learning and of cognitive and personal development.

Thinking and writing are essentially solitary work; but the solitude is peopled by teachers, colleagues, students, friends, and antagonists — some met only through reading—whose imagined responses or quiet presence shape that thinking and writing. Some of the main influences on this study are sketched in the Preface. Carol Chomsky's enthusiasm helped nurture it from its beginnings and sustain its growth. Without Jeanne Chall, Bill Perry, my husband, and my son, there would have been no study at all.

This work was furthered by a scholarship from the New England Reading Association.

Except in the form of an individual person's reading a particular text or writing a particular message in a specific situation, reading and writing do not exist. "Reading" and "writing" are abstractions, convenient abbreviations enabling us to *refer* to certain kinds of human activities. These terms can also lead us to believe that what they refer to has a concrete existence. For example, we are told the "reading" level of various groups of children, although *groups* do not read. Only individuals read. We are not told what these individuals have been asked to read or under what conditions, nor are we reminded that "reading" tests can only indirectly measure "reading." Unless we keep reminding ourselves that "reading" and "writing" are abstractions and abbreviations, we may come to believe—or, just as dangerously, to act as though we believed—in their disembodied existence.

Furthermore, someone reads or writes something *for some purpose.* We do not read for the sake of reading, nor write for the sake of writing. Consider why you are reading this now. "Reading" and "writing" are meaningless as well as disembodied if they are regarded as ends in themselves, not as means of learning, imagining, communicating, thinking, remembering, and understanding.

We cannot always specify who is reading or writing what under what conditions and for what purpose—but we sometimes must, to bring us back to the only concrete reality there is. Grade levels, test scores, and statistical analyses of "reading" and "writing" are very abstract—are abstractions about abstractions—although they may appear reassuringly tangible. Only individuals read and write particular messages, under particular conditions.

Contents

Illustrations

Part One
Writing

1 Paul: Invented Spelling

The Beginning of Invented Spelling (5:1-5:3)

Five-year-old Paul was in the house. I was outside on the deck reading. After he had tried unsatisfactorily to talk with me, he decided to get my attention a new way — to break through print with print. Selecting the rubber letter stamps he needed from his set, Paul printed and delivered this message: RUDF (Are you deaf?!). Of course, I put down my book.

He could put *his* words on paper. Since literacy has become commonplace, we do not often wonder at the power of the written word, except as we may see a child come into the power that was once the secret of the priests. For the next month Paul wrote avidly, developing an alphabetic spelling system that served his needs, and producing a variety of forms (signs, captions, notes, statements, lists, directions, a game, and a story). Before looking ahead to this development in writing, we will look back at conditions and events that seem to have led up to it.

Paul lived in a house that was full of print, and he frequently saw his parents reading and writing. We had read aloud to him almost nightly since he was old enough to enjoy a story (some time between one and two years of age), and he had a collection of his own books. He had sets of wooden letters, magnetic letters, and rubber letter stamps. His family had given him no instruction in letter sounds or letter formation, though letter names were frequently referred to.

He had watched "Sesame Street" since he was three years old. At four, he knew the sounds of some consonants and named the initial letter of several spoken words; he wrote his own name (which no one remembers teaching him); he formed letters and enjoyed writing them. Paper, pencil, crayons, magic markers, and the family typewriter were readily available to Paul. An only child living in the country, he had stretches of solitude that may have encouraged him to develop his own resources and that enabled him to concentrate without external distractions.

His first writing—that is, use of letter forms to represent a message—occurred several months before the RUDF incident, when he inscribed a "welcome home" banner for me that looked like this (actual size 1' by 4'):

Next, he typed strings of letters which he described as notes to his friends. Then he produced a handwritten message—large, green letters to cheer me up when I was feeling low:

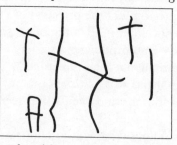

These first, occasional writings spanned several months, during which time he showed an interest in handwriting.

Paul moved from using letters to convey a general message to using letters to spell words when he set up a bookstore (5:1).

He copied the book titles on a sheet of paper, asked how to spell "prices," which he wrote, and then added R 3 5 and some other numbers (prices are 3¢, 5¢, and so on). On a printed ticket that had "No." and then a blank space on it, Paul wrote in the figure *1* : No. 1. "Oh, number one," I said. "No," Paul corrected, "no one."

At this time he was showing an increased interest in reading, in trying to figure out words. He was able to identify most of the book titles on his list, given quite a few seconds to look at them. Only when I asked him the price of *The Day of the Wind* did he have to pick up the book and hold it next to his list to locate the title and price there. When I asked him how he knew which word on his book list said "circus," he said, "Because the last letter was a *s*." He expressed his understanding of the relationship between reading and spelling about a month later, soon after printing RUDF: "Mother, once you know how to spell something, you know how to read it." From then on he wrote prolifically and steadily for a month, and his writings became his reading materials.

Paul was familiar with lowercase as well as capital letter forms when he started spelling; his use of capitals expresses a preference that has been observed in other young writers. Söderbergh's child (1971, p. 126), having learned to read from lowercase words, then began to write in capitals. John, the early reader and writer studied by Torrey (1973), printed in capitals wherever possible although he could write and read lowercase letters. Paul often transcribed to capitals when copying words printed in lowercase. His first year of writing involved little direct copying of letter forms or words, in contrast to most school writing programs.

Capital letter forms are more distinctive than lowercase letters, retaining their identity even when reversed. (In fact, the Greeks, who wrote from left to right, reversed the alphabet they borrowed from the Phoenicians, who wrote from right to left; and this reversed alphabet is the basis of our capital letters.) Lowercase letters were a much later development, not established until the fifteenth century. More than a third of the lowercase letters (n, u, h, y, m, w, b, d, p, q) depend for their distinctiveness on position in space (orientation plus vertical relation to a baseline)—a dimension young children do not control as easily as distinctiveness by shape alone. The positioning of capital letters can be more irregular without obliterating their uniqueness. Adult use of capitals for important communications (headlines, telegrams, signs) and for ease of identification (on typewriter keys and alphabetical indexes) seems to confirm their visual primacy and the conventional wisdom of familiarizing children with them first.

Just as in the historical evolution of writing systems, writing was not originally a way of encoding speech but a separate system, so Paul's first writings were not attempts to spell but to print letters with a communicative intent—the banner to welcome me home from a trip, the strings of letters typed as notes to friends (never sent), and the page of green letters to make me "feel better." In order to approximate our alphabetic orthography, Paul needed to master letter formations, the left-to-right, top-to-bottom spatial and sequential arrangement of print, and the principle that letters have sounds which are used to represent the sounds in words.

When Paul asked how to spell a sound or a word, his father and I responded with the requested information, as we did when he asked for help in reading. Sometimes, when it seemed he could answer his own question, we turned it back to him. Letters supplied on request by an adult will be given in boldface type, as in **WAUTH** (wash) and **TECH** (teach). Paul's invented spellings will be printed in capital letters, following the usage in previous research. Capital letters are also the form in which he at first wrote letters by hand. Sometimes he typed, pressing the keys marked with capital letters but producing lowercase forms.

RUDF shows the letter name strategy that Paul shares with other young children who invent their own spellings and use letters to stand for letter names (R = are, and so forth) rather than, as conventionally in spelling, just sounds (Read, 1971). The sounds of most consonants can be found in their letter names, as the "duh" sound in "dee," which Paul used to write DF (d-eff = deaf). Paul may have traced sounds back to letter names or remembered letter-sound associations from "Sesame

Street." Three days after printing RUDF (5:1), Paul typed 4547781 PAULSTLEFNMBR (telephone number) and PAULSBZR (buzzer), each on a separate sheet of paper—a first step in segmentation. The spellings necessarily use letter sounds almost entirely since a letter name occurs only once in these words: the *L* in TLEFN stands for its name. Paul has omitted representation of the vowel sound of "uh" (short *u* and unstressed vowel or schwa, which is not found in any letter name) and of "eh" (short *e*) except for the *E* in TLEFN. He used it again the next day, printing across a sheet of paper lengthwise so that it would all fit on one line: PAULSELEFIT (elephant). This time he did not use any letter name strategy where it was available but instead separately represented the vowel and consonant sounds in EL as well as EF.

While working on another sheet of paper, he said, "I can't find the letter that makes 'sh' " (5:1). I told him and he finished typing PAULSKRW**SH** (car wash, boldface indicating letters supplied on request). He must have known the sound of *w* or he would have represented "wuh" with a *y* from its letter name. During that same writing session he typed PAULSPIIP (pump), omitting the nasal, *m*, before the consonant as the day following he omitted the nasal, *n*, before a consonant in ELEFIT. This omission is characteristic of inventive spellers.

On still another sheet of paper he had typed PAULSBU when he asked me what letter made the "oo" sound. I said two *o*'s, so he crossed out his *U* and finished. When I read BOOL aloud as "bool"—it was intended for "pool"—he saw his mistake and burst into tears. The tears are important, and there were more to come in his struggle with spelling. They are a measure of the intensity of that effort.

Paul produced a prodigious number of handwritten pages, including a five-page story, two days later. His letters were large so that only a few fit in a row across the page. At first he wrote one word per line; then, as his messages lengthened, he filled out the lines with more words, and he divided words between lines. He continued to separate his messages by writing each on a different sheet of paper, except for the story, which was too long. He wrote three lines of story on every page, which filled the space; he numbered the pages and was pleased with my suggestion to bind them together. These are his writings for that day (5:1) in the order he wrote them:

PAULS	PAULS	PAULS	PAULS
FAN	BAT	DP (dump)	GAMP (jump
			ROP rope)

He had asked for the letter making the "guh" sound in order to write "gorilla" but then decided to write "jump rope" instead. The *M* in GAMP is probably due to my having just volunteered that "dump" was spelled d-u-m-p.

DAD		PAULS	
IMGON	(I am going	GABJ	(garbage)
TOOGOO	to go.)		

PAULS		PAULS	
MAKME	(milk ma-	LATRTOO	(letter to
SHIN	chine)	RMAMDE	Mom: Dea-
		RMAM	r Mom)

THES	(This
ESAPE	is a pi-
PKIHRF	picture of
AHAOOS	a house.)

The PE may be a false start on the word "picture," which seems to be completely represented on the next line. As Read (1971) has observed in other inventive spellers, the sound "ch" is found in the name of the letter *h*, which is consequently used to represent it, as here in PKIHR (picture). The following page was a drawing of a house.

This story was written on five pages:

WANS	WAN	AD	AWA	RKA
APNA	SA	THTB	AD E	MBK
TMTAR	BAR	AR WAT	ENAV	AGAN
1	2	3	4	5
(Once	wa-	and	away	er ca-
upon a	s a	that b-	and he	me back
time there	bear	ear went	(he) nev-	again.)

The next day he wrote:

PAULS	BRZ	BRZ
TALAF	KANF	KAN GO
ONBOO**TH**	LIAD	PLASEZ
(teleph-	(Birds	birds
one booth)	can f-	can go
	ly and	places.)

Notice that from this point on Paul never divides words across pages (represented by separate columns). Paul started on a newspaper, which was to include something about Peanuts (he asked me what made an "utz" sound), but junked it in a fit when he made a mistake. Since he wanted to write with pen rather than pencil, and since he did not let mistakes go by, they were disastrous and accompanied by tears. He also folded over a sheet of paper to make a birthday card illustrated on the cover and inscribed inside:

HAB	(Happy	5 YE	5 yea-
BRTH	birth-	RZ	rs
DA	day	OD	old.)

And he left this note on his play house:

IEA	(I ha-	STOR	store.)
VGAW	ve go-		
NTOOTHE	ne to the		

These two days of intense absorption in writing occurred over a weekend when he was home all day. During the next week he produced a board game with animal names:

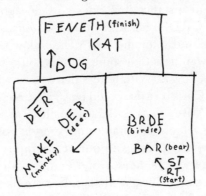

He typed, again on separate sheets of paper:

IHAVATWALVMAKR (I have a twelve-maker.)

DONTGATNERABEHIV (Don't get near a bee hive.) I heard
him sounding this out letter by letter at the typewriter.

DOTGATNERA KOR! (Don't get near a car!) Paul asked me
what made the "ah" sound, and not knowing the word he had
in mind, I supplied the *O* in KOR. The exclamation point,
whose expressive function he quickly grasped, was the first
punctuation mark he used—and continued using with gusto.

EFUDOTBSELEIWELGUAPRRZET (If you don't be silly I
will give you a present.)

PAULZCIDERMUSHEN (cider machine) with a drawing of
the machine. Before writing this, Paul had seen the "cider"
label on a bottle and tried to remember the spelling. "C-i-d-
d-" he said, and then I brought out the bottle for him to copy
from the label.

He did not ask me how to spell "machine," but how to spell
the "uh" and "sh" sounds. This was the characteristic form of his
requests for information about spelling; he was spelling
primarily sounds rather than words at this stage. When he
asked for the spelling of a vowel sound that had several common spellings, I sometimes asked what word it was in, out of
my own awareness of context dependence. My questions did
not immediately alter the form of Paul's; he still continued to
ask how to spell isolated sounds. Sometimes I was sensitive
enough to his spelling system to be content with giving him a
common spelling pattern whether it was correct in a particular
word or not. For instance, his "out of order" signed looked like
this: **OWTUVORDR**, because I told him *o-w* as a spelling for
the "ow" sound and *u* for the "uh." The following week he articulated his awareness that some sounds could be represented
by alternate spellings: "With letters there's two ways of spelling
some words." "Cat," he said, could be spelled K-A-T or C-A-T,
and "baby" B-A-B-Y or B-A-B-E. Thus he was aware early in
his spelling development that some sounds could be represented by alternate spellings in our orthography.

When I asked why he now wrote "Paul's" with a *Z* instead of
his usual *S,* he said, "Because it sounds more like a z-z-z." I do
not know where his original *S* spelling came from; no one had

apparently taught it to him. Other changes in the spellings of words that Paul repeated during these first two weeks of intensive writing document Carol Chomsky's notion (1970) of reinvented spellings. The child is not memorizing words but rather figuring out the spelling of each word, even those written previously, as a new problem; consequently he is not learning "misspellings" by repetition. Paul wrote TLEFN (telephone) but three days later spelled it TALAFON; KR (car) but a week later **KOR**; and BRZ (birds) but the next day BRDE (birdie). The later spellings represent the sounds in these words more fully and with less use of letter name strategy (AL instead of L for "el" in "telephone," and OR instead of R for "ar" in "car").

I am documenting here everything I recorded that Paul wrote during his first weeks as an inventive speller to try to convey the rapid flourishing and evolution of that development. Does merely presenting all these writings convey Paul's absorption in the activity—the hours of intense concentration over pen and paper, or sitting at the typewriter? He was not playfully experimenting but focusing so earnestly on his self-set task of putting language into print that the house was at once hushed and electrified by the tension, with its triumphs and tears.

We return to Paul at the end of his second week of spelling as he presents me with this typed message:

EFUKANOPNKAZIWILGEVUAKANOPENR (5:2)

He might not have arrived at spacing between words as early in his writing as he did without my intervention out of bewilderment at this chain of words. He read it aloud to me ("If you can open cans, I will give you a can opener"), pointing to the appropriate letters and pausing between words; so I mentioned that many writers put spaces between words. He said something like, "I know, but you didn't tell me before," and typed:

EFU W**AU**TH KLOZ I WEL GEVUA WAUTHEN-
MATHEN
(If you wash clothes I will give you a washing machine.)

This was not the first time he asked how to spell the "aw" sound (as in "cr*aw*l" and in his pronunciation of "w*a*sh") even though it occurs in his own name which he had written numerous times, but written apparently as an ideograph rather than an alphabetic representation of the spoken word. Another instance of name perceived as ideograph, not part of the code, is a child I know of who had difficulty in reading words like "night" and "light," although his name was Dwight!

Next Paul typed:

IWAT2 GOTOTHADEN
(I want to go to the [gar]den.)

"What makes the 'ah' sound?" he asked. And then answered himself before I could, "Oh, I know — A-U." I reminded him that *a-u* made "aw" and said he needed only an *a*.

Three days later, without any further word from me about spacing, Paul typed a page arranged like this:

I WIL TE**CH** U T**O** RIT AD THES EZ HA**OW** U RIT
KAT BAT MAT DOG RAKET **ROWBOW** T LOLEPOP
M**OP** D**O**DO DUMDUM BOOBBEE RESAS
MUPS BLAKS DOEN WEPRWEL
(I will teach you to write and this is how you write
cat, bat, mat, dog, racket, rowboat, lollipop,
mop, dodo, dumdum, booby, recess,
mumps, blocks, doing, whippoorwill.)

While writing this Paul had asked many questions about spelling; sometimes he asked for the spelling of isolated sounds, sometimes he gave me a word context (" 'ah' like in 'mop' "), and sometimes he asked for the spelling of words. The form of his questions was changing, perhaps in response to my concern about context, but also because he had chosen to write a spelling lesson and thus focus on isolated words rather than sounds in sentences. His choice of this form is, of course, indicative of his development. Here is the dialogue that accompanied the writing:

Paul:	What makes the "ch"? (in TE*CH)*
Mother:	*c-h.*
Paul:	What makes "oo"?
Mother:	*o-o.*
Paul:	In "to."
Mother:	Only one *o.*
Paul:	What makes the "oo" in "how"? (pronounced hah-oo)

Mother:	*o-w.*
Paul:	How do you spell "row"?
Mother:	*r-o-w.*
Paul:	How do you spell "boat"?

I understood him to say "bow," so I answered: *b-o-w.* (He added on the T anyway: ROWBOW T.)

Paul:	How do you make 'ah' in "lolly"?
Mother:	*o.*

Paul asked again about the "ah" in "pop" and in the next word "mop," and was answered with *o.*

Paul:	What makes an "uh" sound? (DUM)
Mother:	Usually a *u.*
Paul:	What makes the "oo" sound? (BOOBBEE)
Mother:	*o-o.*
Paul:	What makes the "uh" sound?
Mother:	In what word?
Paul:	"Mumps."
Mother:	*u.*
Paul:	What makes the "ah" sound, in "block"?

I understood him to say "blah" so I answered *a,* and he spelled it BLAKS.

Paul:	How do you spell "do"?
Mother:	That just has one *o.*

A few days later (still 5:2) Paul announced, "I figured out two ways to spell 'if.' You can spell it E-F or I-F." When I asked if he knew which way most people spelled it, he said I-F. He was starting to write:

IFU LEV AT **THRD**	(If you live at Third
STRET IWEL **KOM** TO **YOR**	Street I will come to your
HAWS	house.
THE ED	The end.)

This was handwritten, the main message printed on the first three lines of a sheet of ruled paper, with a large THE ED spanning several lines beneath it. "See how small I can write," said Paul proudly. He also wrote:

THES EZ A RIT	(This is a writ-
EN KAS	ing class.)

He was writing less prolifically now. Several days elapsed again before he typed:

THES EZ PAULZ FOLDR

and then folded the paper over to look like a "folder"—his most realistic referent yet. His asking how to write the "oh" sound may show how far he was from a letter name spelling strategy at this point and also his awareness of the variability of vowel sound spellings.

Three days later Paul used writing again to identify and describe a tangible object, in contrast to his imaginary "milk machine," "twelve-maker," and so forth. He typed on a piece of birch bark:

WE FA **OU** D THES AT SPR **U** S MA **OUT** EN
(We found this at Spruce Mountain.)

The spacing perhaps reflects the units in which he encoded the words; however, the following day Paul used conventional spacing in typing a letter:

DER **JENCHAL** I M EN KIDRGARDEN AD I KAN RIT
(Dear Jeanne Chall, I am in kindergarten and I can write.)

When I asked him about putting his name on the letter, he first said he was going to write "from Paul," then he changed to "Paul wrote that above"; but what he finally typed, above the letter he had already written, was PAUL ROT THES. Then he started to write a song book, the first of many little books he was to write through all the succeeding years of this study. It was never completed, though, because of some mistake that made him burst out with "Oh, I fucked up everything," and throw the paper in the wastebasket. "I wanted to write a song book," he wailed. Three days later (5:2) his writing spurt ended with a typed sign:

MAN WRKEN WETH BLOKS
(Men working with blocks.)

While writing the song book, Paul observed, "You spell 'book' B-O-O-K. To write 'look' you just change one letter—take away the *B* and add an *L*." This mental spelling and word transforming continued after his writing spurt temporarily petered out: "If you took the *L* out of 'glass' and pushed it all together, you'd have 'gas'," he mused while lying in bed. Such manipulation was the form that the next phase of his spelling development took. The following week (5:3) he mentally removed the *L* from "please," leaving "pease" (or "peas" or "pees"), and after we had some conversation about Daedalus and Icarus, observed that "If you put an *L* in front of Icarus, you get 'licorice.' " And "If you take the *T* and *R* off of 'trike' and put a *B* in front, you have 'bike.' "

Paul had written some words in kindergarten one day while the other children were drawing pictures. When he brought the paper home and looked at FIER AJEN (fire engine), he commented that FI backwards would be IF — "if-er engine." He also noted that "engine" (AJEN) could have been spelled with a *G*.

He also sometimes included a spelled-out word in his conversation; for example, "I am N-O-T going to pick carrots" (5:3) and "Does anyone have any money for my B-A-K?" (bank) (5:4). Once he attempted spelling an entire sentence. His eyes periodically rolled up while he was keeping track of his place in the sequence, as though it was written at the top of his head: NA WATS PU DK ("Nah, what's up, Doc?"). He must have sensed his reversal of "up" for he asked me if it was right, I corrected it, and he spelled the whole sentence through again: NA WATS UP DK (5:5).

Before moving on to the next phase in Paul's writing development, we will pause to reflect on what he has already learned and accomplished. As a writer, Paul has explored many of the literary forms he will use and elaborate during the next almost five years. He has written:

signs — e.g., OWT UV ORDR (out of order)
lists — e.g., book price list
informative notes — e.g., DADIMGONTOOGOO (Dad, I am going to go.)
letters — e.g., PAULS LATR TOO MAM (Paul's letter to Mom)
labels and captions — e.g., PAULZCIDERMUSHEN
a story — WANS APNA TM
a greeting card — HAB BRTH DA
a game — board game with animal names on spaces
directions — I WIL TECH U TO RIT
statements — e.g., BRZ KAN FLI (Birds can fly.)

Paul also attempted a newspaper and a book. To some extent he seemed to be practicing the forms rather than using them for their intended adult purposes. His note "I have gone to the store" was only pseudo-informative; he had not gone at all. His "out of order" sign referred to nothing that was out of order, as I recall. Most of what looked like descriptive labels—like "Paul's telephone booth"—applied to no known object. The birthday card was simply *made,* not made for any particular occasion or person (though it was for someone who, like its creator, was five years old). "Paul's letter to Mom: Dear Mom" was all form and no content. The forms were conventional, but the purposes often were not. Fanciful notions were conveyed in factual-sounding forms ("I have a twelve-maker"). As Vygotsky said, summarizing Piaget, "Up to the age of seven or eight, play dominates in child thought to such an extent that it is very hard to tell deliberate invention from fantasy that the child believes to be the truth" (Vygotsky, 1962, p. 13). Paul's captions, however, sometimes did go with a picture or object, and a form like a story has no immediate referent or practical purpose.

Although Paul's earliest writings (welcome home banner, green letters, RUDF note) were clearly expressive and directed to a particular audience, his next writings usually defied classification as informative or expressive, or as written for a particular audience. Paul was eager to show me and his father what he had written, and we were pleased with it; but he was not working that hard just to please us. *His* purpose at this stage seemed to involve competence, mastery, control. He was writing to learn to write. The forms he chose for this practice were not, however, irrelevant to his development as a writer, reader, and person, as will be evident later in this study.

The diversity not only of literary forms, but of grammatical forms and vocabulary in Paul's early writing contrasts with the highly structured and repetitive nature of many school programs for beginning writers. The only frame he used repeatedly was "Paul's ————." Looking back on this as a nine-year-old, Paul speculated that it was because he had just learned to write his name—a logical theory, but he knew how to write his name months before this. The emphasis should be on the fact that it was *his* name, for he did not repeat most other words he had written. With no external demands for neat letter forms, proper spacing, writing on the line, or conventional spelling (and apparently only moderate internal demands, plus help from the typewriter), Paul was free to determine whatever he wanted to write and then figure out how to do it. When he was faced with these demands in school a year later, his style became more restricted.

Before formal instruction in first grade, however, Paul was moving toward conventional spacing and spelling. When I told him that many writers put spaces between words, how did he know where to put these spaces — an automatic operation for a literate adult, but for a child who is not actually reading yet? How much of our awareness of words as separate units derives from our seeing them that way in print? Since the boundaries between words are not marked by pauses in speech, how does a pre-reader determine them? Studies of preschool and kindergarten children indicate that they have difficulty separating words presented in phrases or sentences; the superiority of first graders on segmentation tasks may result from their experience with the printed word. Paul had a lot of exposure to print and was attempting to read, mainly through context plus initial or final letter cues, at the time he began segmenting in writing. Whether his awareness of word boundaries came primarily from print is not evident.

Two incidents a few months later (5:6) suggest that his concept of a word — or at least of a noun — related to its correspondence with an object. Looking at a Strawberry Ice Cream Gum wrapper, Paul read "ice" but could not read "cream." When I told him what the word was he said, "I didn't know 'cream' was a separate word from 'ice.' " In typing his name he mistakenly ran his first and last names together, but decided that was all right because he was "all one," indicated by a sweeping gesture up and down his body.

This same month, during his second writing spurt, Paul wrote A PAN A TIM. What but our familiarity with how these words *look* tells us that "upon" has a different structure than "a time"? Listen to them: upon a time. For someone whose experience with language has been mostly auditory, they *sound* like two article + noun strings. Even if one thinks about their meaning — which is less likely in a formulaic phrase — "upon" does not make a lot of sense. Paul's writing of A PAN A TIM points to his use of sound patterns to determine segmentation.

As for some of the fundamental regularities of our writing system, Paul, like other inventive spellers, distinguished vowel and consonant letters and sounds from the start; that is, he never put a consonant or a vowel letter in the place of the other, though he sometimes omitted vowels when the needed vowel sound was included in a consonant name, as in "el" (TLEFON [telephone]). Most often and persistently he omitted the vowel, as Read reports other inventive spellers do, in the presence of vocalic *r* and *l*: LATR (letter), LETL (little). Again like other inventive spellers described in the research, Paul mastered the consonants first, using them to represent the stable sounds they generally do in English. After the first week, his spellings usually included a vowel in each syllable — another basic principle of English orthography — with the exception noted above.

Learning English orthography was not Paul's concern at this point in his spelling history. He was not after correctness but rather phonemic transcription — finding some way of representing for himself the significant sounds he distinguished in words. His first questions were all about which letters made particular sounds: "What letter makes the 'uh' sound?" He could isolate the sounds, but particularly when these sounds were not contained in any of the letter names, he had to improvise or ask. The seven consonantal sounds of English not included in our letter names are exemplified in the italicized segments of the following words: *th*in, *th*en, *g*ot, *sh*ip, trea*s*ure, runni*ng*, *h*ope. Paul asked for all but the last three. He asked as well about vowels and diphthongs. Most of these questions were asked repeatedly, and although in the first week he grappled with the spellings pretty much by himself, after that hardly a page was written without his asking the letter for some sound during the first month of invented spelling.

He worked hard at analyzing sounds, making finer distinctions as he went along and figuring out letter correspondences where he could, so I freely gave most of the information he asked for. Had he requested mainly the spellings of words

rather than sounds, I—like first grade teachers who want to encourage invented spelling—might have withheld information.
The kind of information Paul asked for was the kind that led
him most rapidly to independence in spelling. Some of this information he absorbed immediately (for instance, he asked only once for the letter that made the "guh" sound) and some he
had to request again and again (as the *th* spelling). Obviously,
he was learning on his own schedule and not as a function of
the number of times he was told something.

I have wondered if I presented him with too much information about the complexity of vowel spellings. When Paul asked
for the letters of a vowel or diphthong sound that had multiple
spellings, I often asked him what word the sound was in before
giving an answer. I do not know whether my implication that
spelling depended on the word context and not just on the
isolated sound perpetuated his dependence on adult help in
spelling during the first two months he was writing. However,
Paul himself had operated almost from the start on the principle that one letter can represent different sounds. In one day
during his first week of spelling he independently used *A* for six
different sounds:

WANS *once*	AWA *away*
BAR *bear*	MAM *mom*
AD *and*	MAK *milk*

Consistently he used *A* to represent the greatest variety of
vowel sounds, although he increasingly used the other vowel
letters for more than one sound each. During his first month of
invented spelling, he commented that *O* sometimes makes an
"oo" sound, as in "to." This strategy resulted, of course, from
the existence of many fewer vowel letters than vowel sounds in
English.

Very early in his spelling Paul became aware of one source of
irregularity in English orthography: the fact that one sound
may have several different representations. This is the only
such orthographic principle he articulated. "With letters there's
two ways of spelling some words" (CAT or KAT, BABY or
BABE, EF or IF, AJEN or AGEN).

Paul used the principle that a combination of letters may

represent a single sound, though he did so only after being told
two-letter spellings for some sound, such as "oo" and "th". Since
th is perhaps the most frequent digraph in English orthography
it was, logically, the first one Paul mastered. He used it for
months to represent the sound "sh" as in WAU*TH*EN-
MA*TH*EN as well as for both sounds of *th* (all sounds he could
differentiate) — the principle of one representation for several
sounds again.

Thus as a beginning speller, Paul showed at least a working
knowledge of the main sources of variability in English orthography: different letters representing a single sound, a
single letter representing different sounds, and a combination
of letters making a single unique sound.

How did Paul's work on "phonics" through invented spelling
during the period of this first writing spurt and subsequent oral
spelling activity — about four months in all — affect his reading
ability? As already mentioned, his writing was preceded by a
noticeable interest in reading, in the sense of word identification. At first he was not sounding words out fully but using a
combination of beginning and final letter clues and context to
recognize — not decode — anticipated words, such as his name
in a paragraph I had written, book titles on his list, and labels
on food packages. His own writings then became his reading
materials. When the writing tapered off, he tried reading
printed materials again: largely cereal boxes and selections
from books. He only once tried to read the main text of a book,
but rather chose captions and signs included in illustrations.
Since the illustrations often did not provide sufficient context
clues to identify the words, his reasons for choosing captions
and signs probably related to their shortness (he was reading
very slowly) and to the preference for such forms that showed
in his own writings. He was now, after that month of intensive
invented spelling and some oral spelling manipulations, coming to use a decoding strategy more fully for reading.

Paul's interest in language had another dimension during
this period: his curiosity about the reasons for names. This
sometimes came out in the form of questions, for instance asking why "witchgrass" and "hamburger" were so called. "Hamburger" particularly puzzled him because he knew a ham-

burger did not contain ham. He knew that "silverware" was
called "silver" because of its color, but why was it called "ware"?
Sometimes he had solved the puzzle: "I know why they're called
'Cheerios.' Because they're shaped like *o*'s and they make you
feel sort of cheery" or "That's why it's called 'ice cream' — because it's cream made into ice."

His intellectual interests were not just in language areas.
The bookstore, which involved him in his first sustained
writing activity, was the first of many business projects
developed over the next five years. Often these entailed considerable writing. Construction projects, which absorbed him
as his first writing spurt faded, have been a strong and enduring interest. Writing was to become a part of these projects
during his next writing spurt. Numbers intrigued him before
he started spelling and have been a recurrent interest, later
becoming incorporated into the lists and charts Paul wrote.

Independent Invented Spelling (5:3-5:9)

After the interlude of oral spelling and word transformations, Paul returned to writing again, at first through occasional signs and notes that were truly informative or related to
a concrete context:

> OPEN and KLOZD signs for his bookstore
> IM GOING TOMATHUZ HAO (S omitted)
> (I am going to Matthew's house.)

When I read IM as "I'm" Paul corrected me: "I am." He
likewise read "I'm" in books as "I am." He did not ask for any
information about spelling — an independence characteristic of
this second spelling phase. Previously he had represented -*ing*
with N or EN: GON (going), RITEN (writing), and, in his
pronunciation, the similar sounding ending of OPN or OPEN.
Several weeks ago I had mentioned the -*ing* spelling to him, and
perhaps his reading had reinforced it since then, so he now
wrote GOING.

> FOR HANRE FRAM PAUL on a gift to his father, Henry.
> AUOT and AOT AV ORDR signs for machines he had built.

Although I had earlier supplied *u* several times as a spelling for
the "uh" sound, Paul now used *A*, as in AV (of), consistently for

the next several months. Just being told a spelling was not sufficient condition for remembering. The *A* for "uh", which Beers and Henderson (1977) report as a late development in their young spellers, may come from reading — from the unstressed pronunciation of the article "a."

About three months after the end of his first writing spurt, Paul became fully engaged in writing again (5:6). The most striking change was his independence in spelling. He had worked out a system by which he could represent satisfactorily to himself the sounds of the language. This mastery and independence almost brought an end to the devastating moments of tearful frustration over errors that had characterized his earlier efforts. When he did ask questions, they were usually about the spelling of *words* rather than *sounds*. I wish I had recorded whether he stopped sounding out words aloud as he wrote during this period; my impression is that he came to write silently. If so, he had internalized the sounds, for his invented spellings were highly phonemic.

Paul wrote steadily for three months (5:6 through 5:8), developing most of the forms he had written in before, refining his invented spelling to a more complete and readable phonemic system, and spelling an increasing number of words conventionally. A representative selection from Paul's writings is presented here; the order is only roughly chronological.

During the first month he most frequently wrote signs, which became part of his construction and play activities:

PAULZ. HOS. PLANF.ELD. VRMAT
(Paul's house, Plainfield, Vermont)

This is Paul's first use of dots for segmentation. He wrote almost everything by hand at this time (5:6), and spacing between words — which had been easy enough on the typewriter — probably required more anticipation of word length and control of handwriting than the dot system. The use of periods to separate words was Paul's reinvention of an ancient device, refining an even earlier manner of writing, which Paul, like his ancient forebears, had started from: "In the earliest manuscripts the text is usually written continuously without separation of words . . . In some early manuscripts words are

separated by dots" (Ullman, 1969, p. 211). During the next two
months Paul extended the dot system to segmenting compound
words, affixes, and sometimes even syllables: AFTR.NUN
(afternoon), JAN.S (Juan's), FOR.GAT (forget), RAN.ENG
(running), TAL.A.FON (telephone), RA.T.O. (radio).
Another reinventor of the dot system, six-year-old Denver, has
been observed by Harste, Burke, and Woodward (forthcoming).

Other signs Paul wrote during this time are described in
chronological order:

PAULZ RABR SAF RABRZ KANT GT EN
(Paul's robber safe. Robbers can't get in.)

This sign was posted on the door of his cabinet. Extensive
maneuvers against "the robbers" engaged Paul and his good
friend Matthew for several years. The next two signs announced his independence. The first was posted over his work-
bench:

DO NAT DSTRB GNYS AT WRK
(Do not disturb. Genius at work.)

and the second, on the door to his room:

DO.NAT KM.IN.ANE.MOR.JST.LETL.KES
(Do not come in anymore. Just little kids.)

The following signs were on block constructions he and a friend
had built:

THA.BEG.EST HOS.EN.THA.WRALD
(The biggest house in the world.)
KI.ING.AV.THA.WRALD
(King of the world.)

Later that day he wrote KING on one side of a banner and
KI.ING on the other. Paul systematically did not represent the
reduced vowel sound before *r* (DSTRB, WRK); but in
WRALD he represents the intervocalic *r* he would hear in
slowly sounding out "world," making it two syllables with the *r*
sound in the first one: "wer-uld."

Paul's writing became utterly integrated with the block play
activities as he came to write directly on the blocks rather than

on paper attached to them. He inscribed STRT and FENETH (start, finish) on the blocks at either end of a race track he built, and FYOS BOX (fuse box) to identify a single block. During his first invented spelling phase, Paul had asked repeatedly how to spell the "th" sounds. Early in this second phase, he overgeneralized the TH spelling he had finally learned, using it to represent "sh" as in FENETH, "ch" as in THANL (channel), and "zh" as in TARATHR (treasure).

Paul continued writing notes and letters to his family and spent hours writing valentines for his friends, unlike the earlier birthday card for no one in particular. He wrote another story, though this time it was only a story in form; the content was a factual description of his dog. Each line below represents one line of Paul's handwriting and each column a page:

WANS.A.PAN	AND.
A.TIM.THR.	HEZ.NAM.WAZ.TADY.
WAZ.A.DOG.	AND.HE.LEVD.EN.PANF
	ELD.VRMANT
(Once upon	and
a time there	his name was Teddy
was a dog	and he lived in Plainf-
	ield, Vermont.)

Compare this, written at 5:6, with the story that five months earlier he had sprawled over five pages:

WANS	WAN	AD	AWA	RKA
APNA	SA	THTB	AD E	MBK
TMTAR	BAR	AR WAT	NAV	AGAN
(Once	wa-	and	away	er ca-
upon a	s a	that b-	and he	me back
time there	bear	ear went	nev-	again.)

In five months of invented spelling Paul had moved from a semisyllabic writing system based on letter names as well as sounds to an alphabetic system in which finer sound distinctions were represented. Historically, this has also been the development of writing systems; the phonetic principle was expressed first through syllabic scripts and later through alphabetic scripts. "The syllabaries already had signs for single vowels, since these could constitute syllables on their own. But it was a remarkable discovery that led to signs for single consonants, because it involved the abstraction of the consonant from the syllable. The sound of *a* can exist by itself, but not the sound of *k*: the consonant requires a vowel with it, making *ak* or *ka*. The sound of the consonant is inseparable from that of the vowel, but the alphabet separates it in writing" (Moorhouse, 1953, pp. 21-22).

As progress toward a complete representation of phonemes, compare these early (5:1) and later (5:6) spellings: TM with TIM (time), E with HE, APN with A.PAN (upon), AD with AND, and WAT (went) with VRMANT (Vermont). Paul has come to represent nasals before consonants (A*N*D, VR-MA*N*T), to include vowel letters in syllables (T*I*M, A.P*A*N), and to move away from letter name strategy (*H*E).

Like this "once upon a time" form embodying factual content, other instances of unconventional use of forms persisted. Here is an announcement of a non-event:

IM.GON.TO.KAT.MI.KAN WETH.SAM.TAKS.AND.
SEZRZ.
AND.IM.GON.TO.DO.ET.TAMARO
(I am going to cut my can with some tacks and scissors
and I am going to do it tomorrow.)

and one of several pseudo-shopping lists:

SHAP.ING.LETS. (shopping list)
5000 BATLZ.AV.WESKY. (bottles of whiskey)
AND 100 BATLZ.AV.BER. (bottles of beer)
AND. 5000 BAGZ.AV.DOG FOD (bags of dog food)

At this time Paul enjoyed producing and naming large numbers on a calculator.

He continued to write labels and captions, although now they always accompanied a picture. Some subjects came from his immediate experiences, such as:

TADE LORES BESEX (Teddy Lawrence Bissex), our dog
CAR. SAAB our car. Evidence that he was picking up some sight words.
THE.TO.PANE.CRCIS (The Two Penny Circus), performers we had seen.

Some were fanciful like:

TIK.TAK.TO. TETHR (tic tac toe teacher)
BANA. TLA.FON (banana telephone)

Most of what he wrote during this period was illustrated, as it was for the next several years, with greater attention sometimes focused on the pictures than on the writing.

Paul continued to write instructional material — directions for how to do things, like the Indian war dance:

HAU.TO.DO.TH.ENDEN.WOR.DANS
FRST.U.TAK WAN.AV.UOR.FET.
(How to do the Indian war dance.
First you take one of your feet . . .)

The directions were understandably not finished. Instead of going through the dance movement by movement, Paul apparently decided to draw a picture of an Indian dancing with lots of zig-zag lines around the legs to convey the energetic motion. His use of the letter *U* in his spellings here is interesting. Since the beginning of his invented spelling (RUDF) he has used *U* to stand for its letter name. Very early he tried using it to stand for the "oo" sound which is part of its name, but he hesitated and asked me for the "oo" sound in "pool," crossing out his *U* and putting in my *O-O*. That *O-O* spelling stuck with him (TOO, HAOOS, BOOTH), later becoming reduced to *O* (TO, HAOS). Here, during his independent invented spelling phase, he uses *U* for that "oo" again in a word he has not written before — "how," pronounced "ha-oo," = HAU — but not in TO or DO, which seem to have become automatic by now. His spelling UOR (your, pronounced "yore") uses the consonantal sound of *y* ("yuh") from the beginning of the letter name "U." Other words containing the "ore" sound (in his pronunciation), he consistently spells with OR: WOR, FOR, MOR, LORENS (Lawrence) and, during his first invented spelling phase, STOR.

Paul wrote directions for running a radio he built of wood scraps (5:8):

DRAKTHENS.FOR.RAN.ENG.MI.RA.T.O.
FOR.TRN.ING.MI.RA.T.O.ON.AND.OFF

YOU.TRN THES *(arrow pointing up)* UP *(arrow pointing up)*
ENTEL.ET.KLEKS (until it clicks)
AND.EF.U.WANT.TO.TRN.ET.OFF.TRN.IT.OFF

Written about two weeks after his Indian war dance instructions, these spellings are for the most part readable phonemic
representations. Paul's unconventional but systematic spellings
of some short vowel sounds are the main barrier to readability.
The short sound of *i* he generally represents by *E* (THES =
this, KLEKS = clicks, EF = if); the short sound of *e* he consistently represents with *A* (DRAKTHENS = directions); and
the short sound of *u* he represents with *A* (RAN = run). UP,
like ON and OFF, must be learned words—learned from
adults or from his own reading—since these spellings are in-
consistent with Paul's other spellings. The "directions for running my radio" include some spellings indicating a new
awareness of standard orthography side by side with invented
spellings: YOU and U, IT and ET. ENG (in RAN.ENG) is a
new invention, alternating here with the conventional ING
form (TRN.ING) that Paul has been using for some time.

During his first writing spurt Paul attempted but did not
complete some sort of newspaper; this time he produced one,
named after our local paper, the *Times-Argus:*

TIMS. R.GIS
THAR.WL.B.SHAWRS. (There will be showers
IN.THE.AFTR.NUN in the afternoon.)
and a picture of RAN. (rain)

Paul might have copied or recalled the spelling of *Times-Argus,*
but instead he invented it. Although he has spelled "car" conventionally for some time, he has not generalized the AR spelling from that learned word; he uses *R,* as here, to represent
both its letter name (R.GIS) and letter sound (AFTR). He has
distinguished the spelling of "sh" (SHAWRS) from "th"
(THAR).

Paul's first "book," his song book, was ill-fated; but during
the latter part of his second writing spurt he wrote four books.
The first was a reminder to me in booklet form:

cover: RAMAMBR.ING. BOOK
p. 1: a long candy bar shape inscribed BIG. BADY (Buddy)
p. 2: DON.T FOR.GAT.THE.BIG.BADY

A is Paul's usual way of representing the short *e* (RAMAMBR) and short *u* (BADY) sounds. He is now representing nasals before consonants, as the second *M* in RAMAMBR.ING.

Next he wrote a spelling book, selecting for instruction only words he could spell conventionally:

SPL.ING. BOOK
P.I.G.SPLS. (drawing of a pig)
B.O.O.K. SPLS. (drawing of a book)
and so on for DOG, CAT, and CAR.

Then a SINGING BOOK.:

NAM .AV.THE.BOOK. TEDY O TEDY
(Some of the letters in the following lyrics were
connected to letters signifying keys on the piano.)
TEDY O.TEDY WIL.U.KAM BAK.
O.PLES.WIL.YOU KAM BAK.SUN
(Oh, please, will you come back soon.)

Paul had originally written SA.**NG** for "song," asking me, in an untypical question for this period of his writing, what made the "ng," which he did not abstract from his knowledge of *-ing*. When he changed the title to "singing," he added the -ING, which he apparently categorizes as an indivisible suffix, as in his earlier KI.ING and, three weeks after the singing book, his spelling SI.ING. I told him to change the *A* in SANG to *I*. At this point he probably would have spelled "sing" SENG, although he occasionally used *I* to represent the short *i* sound.

Paul's spelling of "Teddy" as TEDY is a major change from his earlier TADE. Two days before writing his singing book he had pointed out to his father his change from *A* to *E*, after writing TEDE. On the same paper, however, he spelled "fetches" with an *A,* so the *E* spelling was not yet generalized. A week later, looking at the label on a red raspberry yogurt carton, Paul observed that he had spelled "red" R-A-D, which he pronounced now as "raid." His letter name strategy for spelling the long *e* sound was just beginning to be modified, a process that was very gradual. Paul started, mostly with proper names, using *Y* rather than *E* for a final long *e* sound. His friend Toby had corrected Paul's oral spelling of her name TOBE two weeks before the singing book; Paul had then written TOBY and

KANDYS but also TADE. The next day he had questioned the spelling of his father's name, Henry: "Is it an *E* at the end?" he asked. *Y* and *E* spellings existed side by side for months. A couple of times he overgeneralized the *Y,* spelling "free" FRY and "see" SEY. Later, double-*E* spellings began to appear (BEE, DEER).

As he was finishing his song about Teddy, Paul observed that SUN (soon) said "sun." About three weeks earlier, while writing the last name of a friend, Potter, which Paul had written PATR, he realized "P-A-T spells 'pat.'" "So what would that be?" he asked me. This sort of awareness, stemming from his reading knowledge of words, did not immediately revolutionize his spelling system but surely was one force keeping it moving toward conventional orthography.

While Paul was working on his spelling system, his kindergarten class was being introduced to the "letter people," part of a program to teach the alphabet and letter sounds. His fourth and final book of this period extends and combines his school work with influences from a book I had been reading to him. The kindergarteners had just met "Mr. Z" and were making "Z" books. On his cover Paul had copied from the blackboard: ZIG ZAG ZIPPER BOOK. Inside, he had cut out and pasted some pictures from the "Z" worksheet picture story. The first showed a boy and a girl unhappy over their zigzag zippers. Paul added the following conversation:

girl: MI ZIPPR. WONT ZIP
boy: MIN WONT

On the next page the boy and girl are shown writing letters. Paul added nothing but a page number. Next, Mr. Z is shown with the letters in his hands, saying:

WATe SHAL.I DO I.NOW
(What shall I do? I know.)

Finally, he is shown sewing in a new zipper:

NAW.THAL.BEE.HAPPE
THE ANDe
(Now they'll be happy.
The end.)

The lowercase *e* is Paul's "silent e" and comes from his reading
an "Electric Company" book about "silent e." Apparently he
considers any *e* that does not have a long sound as silent. Inside
the front cover of the book is a dedication: FOR.JAN, and on
the back cover an explanation:

JAN.IS.A.BOY.AND.JAN.S FATHR.ROT.THIS.BOOK.

I had been reading to Paul a book that was prefaced "for Juan"
and had explained that Juan was the author's son.

One of Paul's last writings of this independent invented spelling phase (5:8) was his "report card on sports":

RE.PORT KARD.ON.SPORTS.NAME.PAUL.
PAUL.IS.GOWING.TO.RUN.A.RAWND.AND.JUMP.
AND.EXRSIZ.

After writing this, Paul asked repeatedly if it was all correct.
When I said that I didn't have trouble reading any of the
words, he responded impatiently, "But I want to know if it's all
correct!" This was his first strongly expressed concern for correctness, and his enthusiasm for writing temporarily suc-
cumbed to it. The concern for correctness considerably preceded his entrance into first grade (which subsequently
reinforced it) and followed by a few months the visit of an older
friend who had pointed out Paul's misspellings; it also coincided with a period of great involvement and progress in
reading.

His *awareness* of correct spelling, however, existed before his
concern about it. It was implicit in his questions about how to
spell words and became explicit about the middle of this independent invented spelling phase. While Paul was spelling a
friend's name BAN, he noticed that the friend's older sister
spelled it BEN. After commenting that he thought it was
B-A-N, Paul said to her, "You know what? If something's
wrong with the way I spell, I don't care — I just spell it that way
anyway." Awareness of conventional orthography was certainly behind his "spelling book," and later comparison between his
own spelling RAD and the printed spelling "red." Actually Paul
had been concerned with "correctness" from the beginning, just
a different kind of correctness. During the first phase of invented spelling he assumed there was a correct way to repre-

sent each *sound*. Some of these he felt he knew and others he asked for. "How do you make the 'ah' sound?" implies the existence of just as authoritative an answer as "How do you spell 'again'?" Only the unit of correctness is different. In moving toward *words* as the unit of correctness, Paul was taking another step toward standard orthography. He could represent almost all letter-sound relationships conventionally, but he did not know how letter environment and position in word affected spellings.

In summary, Paul's first attempts to spell soon engaged him in a struggle to work out an adequate representational system. This first period of prolific writing was one of dependent spelling in the sense that he asked many questions about the letters used to represent certain sounds. Then he enjoyed his accomplishments through playful oral spellings, and when he wrote prolifically again, spelled independently. This period of fluent invented spelling gave way to concern for correctness, changing the nature of his questions about spelling from how to spell sounds to how to spell words and whether a word was "spelled right," which probably reduced his writing output. Spellings Paul had learned from reading increased in his writings. The concentration and energy he had focused on spelling now went into reading.

Paul's RE.PORT.KARD. (figure 1) is a measure of his orthographic knowledge at this time, seven months after writing RUDF. When I told Paul that "card" was not spelled with a *k*, he knew it was a *c* instead. Except for words that he must have learned visually, like CAR and CRCIS, he always represented the "kuh" or hard *c* sound with *K*. KARD is the first time, beyond the learned spelling of "car," that Paul has represented the vowel in "ar" rather than just using a letter name strategy (STRT, R.GIS).

When I told Paul that "going" did not have a *w*. he said that he had been thinking of spelling it G-O-I-N-G (as he had spelled it months earlier). This may indicate a fluctuation between phonetic and word analysis spelling strategies. Paul has spelled both "go" and "-ing" conventionally, so he could have just put them together intellectually without listening to the word. When "going" is pronounced, a "wuh" sound can be both heard and felt.

Figure 1.   *"Report card on sports" (5:8).*

Paul's conventional spellings of RUN and JUMP mark a
sudden shift from his previously consistent use of *A* to represent
the short *u* sound. In this case he changed his spelling all at
once; alternate spellings do not exist by side during a transition
period as they did in some other spelling shifts. His representation of the short *i* sound, which underwent such a transition
during much of Paul's second invented spelling phase, is now
almost always spelled conventionally with *I* rather than *E,* as in
IS on his "report card." "Is" Paul had initially spelled EZ. During his first invented spelling phase he distinguished the "s" and
"z" sounds in his spellings: THES EZ (this is), contrary to
Read's observations (1975) on other children. During the second phase he increasingly represented both sounds with *S:* thus
the spelling of "is" changed from EZ to ES and now to IS. As
can be seen on the original of Paul's RE.PORT KARD., he
had first spelled "exercise" with an *S* and then written a large *Z*
over it.

The first word with an "ex" sound in it appeared in Paul's
writing about a month and a half before his "report card":
IKSPLOSIVS, and then a month later NAKS (next). If Paul
had attempted to spell these words early in his invented spelling

development, he might have used the obvious letter name strategy: XPLOSIVS, NX. His use instead of the phonetic KS representation, at a time when he still used a few letter name spellings, may reflect the eclecticism of his approach to spelling (evident from the beginning) as well as his progress in alphabetic spelling. But where did EX come from? Perhaps he had seen the word "exciting." Perhaps it was further evidence of a shift toward conventional spelling of the short *e* sound, which he almost always spelled with *A* but had changed in TEDY and was in the next month to change more frequently to *E*. Perhaps he was able to use his name (Bissex) as a resource for spelling.

Paul had learned about all he could from analyzing sounds and was already beginning to spell morphophonemically and visually. Morphophonemically, he had first learned *-ing* and then he regularized to the conventional *-s* the plural, possessive, and third person present tense markers (SHAWRS, showers; JAN.S, Juan's; SPLS, spells) which he had previously represented by *S* or *Z* according to their sound (TAKS, tacks; SEZRZ, scissors). Since he wrote in the present tense there is no evidence about whether he also represented with a uniform, conventional spelling (*-ed*) the varied pronunciations of the final tense marker (as in lov*ed*, hop*ed*, want*ed*). Visually, words that he had seen were modifying his spellings; for instance, he started spelling "from" conventionally because he had seen it on a card he received. He commented that he used to spell it F-R-*A*-M.

2 Other Young Spellers and Writers

Paul's spelling system was by no means unique. The first research on children's invented spelling was by Read (1970), who investigated invented spellings as evidence of young children's tacit categorizations of English speech sounds. He found a remarkably uniform phonological system among the three- to six-year-olds he studied. These children, before they could read, devised a spelling system based on letter names (KAM = came, STRT = start), on analysis of sounds from letter names (BRD = bird), and on phonetic groupings which often differed systematically from those embodied in English orthography. Children's phonological judgments, he found, are frequently based on place of articulation; for example, lax (or short) vowels are usually represented by the vowel letter whose name contains the closest sound (FLEPR = Flipper, representing short *i* with *E*). Nasals (*m* and *n*) preceding consonants, which are articulated in the same place as the consonants and are not felt as a separate segment, are generally not represented in invented spellings (AD = and, BUP = bump). Read argues that these children, whose spontaneous spellings were already systematically abstract, had learned the principle of spelling. "What the children do not know is the set of lexical representations and the system of phonological rules that account for much standard spelling; what they do know is a system of phonetic relationships that they have not been taught by their parents and teachers" (Read, 1971, p. 30).

Read's central observation of young children's systematic and evolving invented spellings has been supported by subsequent investigators: Carol Chomsky (1971a, 1971b, 1974), Gerritz (1974), Paul (1976), Beers and Henderson (1977). While the research shows some differences in spelling patterns and in sequences of spelling patterns, it concurs on the systematic and abstract nature of the invented spelling process, on the kinds of strategies and categorizations the children employ, on evidence that the spellings progress toward more complete representation of sounds and that the children have no trouble making the transition to conventional spelling when it is required of them.

These researchers have studied preschoolers and first graders, primarily looking for similarities across children's spelling patterns. With their "universals" as a backdrop, this part of my study seeks to present the drama of one child's coming into writing, to document the process and the experience over five years as he gradually masters conventional spelling and matures the forms and purposes of his writing, and to delineate the setting of this drama—the home, the classrooms—and above all the character, activities, and interests of our protagonist, Paul.

Paul himself described what he was doing as "writing" rather than "spelling." "Spelling" he applied to the encoding of individual words, as in his SPL.ING (spelling) BOOK. Had his main interest been in spelling *words,* he would have written word lists; what he wrote, however, were *messages.* He cared about what he wrote, not just about how he wrote it. When we look over six years of his writings, patterns emerge that suggest how much a part of his person and growth his earliest writings were. Therefore this study, while looking closely at Paul's development as a speller, seeks also to keep in view his development as a writer.

Chomsky (1976) and Gerritz (1974) have observed and documented the quality and variety of children's writings in two different first grade classrooms where invented spelling

was encouraged. Children wrote spontaneously and enthusiastically, seemed free to focus on what they were saying
rather than on precise copying tasks, and were able to use the
words they wanted rather than only those they had learned to
spell. In another first grade room where Graves (1979b, 1979c)
observed inventive spellers as they wrote, the productions were
prolific and varied: stories, compilations of information, lists,
signs, menus, letters, and so on. Children spontaneously continued in their writing for more than an hour at a time. In this
first year of writing, Graves sees "a stage of development when
children can make some of the most rapid and delightful
growth in writing of their entire lives" (1979c, p. 2).

Just as we need to recognize differences between children's
and adults' categorizations of speech sounds and representational principles in order to understand children's invented
spelling, so we may need to look beyond the classifications currently used for adult writings in order to understand the forms
and functions of young children's writings. Britton observes
that a good deal of young children's writing "is not aimed at
telling anybody anything but at producing 'written objects' " to
be displayed and preserved (1970a, p. 164). Rosen and Rosen
note:

> The more we examine the writing of children in the primary
> school the clearer it becomes that they do not write out of a
> powerful sense of a particular audience with particular needs
> and, unless the teacher is making special demands, she is no
> more than an added incentive for something which they say for
> the satisfaction of saying. We have seen this to be true even of
> those pieces which seem to be very much audience-directed. It
> becomes more true when children turn over a problem or begin
> to suggest their own ideas about what they have been learning.
> (Rosen and Rosen, 1973, p. 141)

The conventional American classroom distinction between
"creative" and "expository" or "informational" writing is not truly descriptive of young children's writing, according to Rosen
and Rosen:

> As children get older their teachers begin to feel the need to
> shape their development in a very direct way either towards
> "creative" writing or towards informative writing. In either

direction the adult model looms large and sharp differentiation is imposed on children's writing. My own impression has been that the most interesting work throughout the primary school is *relatively* undifferentiated. Restrictive choices and the imposition of a fixed way of treating a theme limit the manoeuvrability of young writers and handicap them in their efforts to explore with language. They must be left free to write in a way which shows how they feel about things. In the process children will write in different ways, but only rarely will they be in conformity with highly differentiated adult models. I say write in different ways, and that puts it rather vaguely but that is because we lack both a theory and the supporting investigation to be more precise about the different forms of writing in the primary school. The terms usually used are totally inadequate. (Rosen and Rosen, 1973, p. 95)

Britton and his associates at the Writing Research Unit in London are also seeking to describe how children's writing develops over time. "Writing is likely to develop from that which relies most closely on the resources of speech (and story) to encompass an increasing range of different kinds" (Burgess et al., 1973, p. 20). In describing writing development, Rosen and Rosen envision a continuum from talk to book language: "The youngest children's writing is nearest to talk though rarely exactly the same as it. Older children who are less sophisticated will tend to stay nearer to talk in their writing than children who read a great deal and become influenced by literary forms and structures" (Rosen and Rosen, 1973, pp. 110-111).

Most of Paul's early writings, by contrast, did not sound conversational. This only began to happen as Paul developed a voice in writing—as a narrator with personality emerged at times at age eight in "A Magic Carpet or Two" and in a more consistent but stylized manner two years later in *Strange* magazine. As Graves has said, "Only advanced writers can make writing sound like speech" (1979b, p. 4). But Graves goes on to describe ways in which the writing of young children who have not yet learned many of the conventions of print *is* close to speech: "When children first write, they treat writing as speech. They draw to supply context for the subject, run words together, spell words as they sound, let words run around the page, speak out loud when they write, blacken in letters, use capitals and exclamation points liberally" (1979b, p. 15). Paul's early writings showed most of these features, although as a ten-year-old editor of *Strange* magazine he still enjoyed expressing vocal gesture graphically—by multiple exclamation points, capital letters, thickened or wobbly lines for letters, and nonlinear letter arrangements. At ten he could, of course, write within the conventions of print but retained some of the graphics as an option.

Drawing tended to be more illustration than context for Paul's writing, even during his first year. Context was more often provided by physical objects, such as the constructions on which he posted his signs. But like other very young writers, he wrote within a context he assumed but never defined, for he had no sense of a removed audience for his writing. Indeed, it was the absence of available context for such early writings as "Paul's telephone booth" or "If you wash clothes I will give you a washing machine" that made them hard to interpret in terms of our usual categories of form and function in writing. The speech of young children likewise *assumes* context, assumes that the listener knows what the speaker knows, and is, in this sense, egocentric.

From his observations of second grade children in four classrooms, Graves concluded that the range and amount of children's writing was inversely proportional to the amount of assigned writing (that is, assigned topics). Girls wrote more in formal classroom environments and on assignment than did boys, for whom "unassigned writing seems to provide an incentive . . . to write about subjects not normally provided in teacher-assigned work" (Graves, 1975, p. 235). Another sex difference Graves noted was in the content of writing, with girls centering more on home and school and taking a personal stance toward their subject, and boys centering more on areas beyond home and school—the larger community, current events, and so forth—from a less personal stance.

Graves's research included case studies as well as observations of large and small groups. On the basis of case studies he concluded that "the writing process is as variable and unique as the individual's personality" (Graves, 1975, p. 237). Pointing to the lack of developmental studies on children's writing, he argues that more direct observation of children and more case studies are needed. "Many of the variables discussed in larger group findings became apparent as a result of the intensive case study. In this sense case studies serve principally as surveying expeditions for identifying the writing territories needing further investigation" (Graves, 1975, p. 239).

Through a case study we see something of the learning processes of many children, although we cannot know how much of what we see is characteristic of only a single child and how much holds true for others until we have looked at others. I have tried to relate research on other children's learning to write, as well as to read, where it intersects with my observations.

Case studies can only disprove the universality of generalizations; we cannot generalize from one case to many. Conversely, we cannot presume to know an individual in terms of generalizations drawn from groups. In our schools, we usually teach to groups, though children (like the rest of us) learn as individuals in the context of groups.

3 Paul: Toward Conventional Spelling

5:10-6:11 (First Grade)

At the same time Paul was refining his invented spelling system, changes in the kinds and numbers of questions he was asking about spelling indicated a shift of attention toward conventional spellings. During his independent spelling phase he had asked how to represent only one sound: "ch" as in "change." In the first month of independent spelling, he had asked questions about spelling two words—"Bissex" and "love"—which he was writing on cards and letters. These were words he could not have spelled correctly using his system, and the fact that they were going to be read by people outside his immediate family may have been an additional cause of his concern for their spelling. In the second month he asked questions about ten words. Only one question was about letters within words: "Is it an *e* at the end of 'Henry'?" Seven questions were requests for spelling entire words: Fred, here, dessert, now, eggs, pet, when—again, all words he could not have spelled conventionally by his system. Two questions were about the correctness of his invented spellings; he wanted to know whether IKSPLOSIVS and HOLDR were "right." During the third and last month of independent invented spelling, the number of questions more than doubled and were mostly requests for entire words.

From 5:10 to 6:3 Paul wrote very little. He did engage in some oral spelling, as he had after his first invented spelling phase, this time as part of a card game he devised. Though set in a game context, the spellings were not playful now, but aimed at correctness. In his original version of the game, players dealt cards off a deck face down, saying a letter with each card until the number or name of a card had been spelled out. A point was scored if the next card, dealt face up, was the one the player had spelled. Since Paul played the game with his parents, he was able to compare his spellings with conventional ones and change them. "Five," "six", "seven," "nine," and "ten" he seemed to know correctly already. His original spelling of W-A-N he changed to O-N-E. His initial spelling of "ace," A-S-S, did not change all at once but in stages, indicating that "silent *e*" was easier for him to assimilate than the notion of *c* making an "s" sound: A-S-S to A-S-E to A-S-C-E to A-C-E. He maintained his T-O-W spelling of "two" in the face of adult models to the contrary, as well as his J-O-K-R-E. Since the conventional spellings of these words contain exactly the same letters as his only in slightly different order, he may not have perceived the difference. Final silent *e* he was ready to accept (JOKRE) but not yet "silent *e*" before *r* (jok*e*r). Paul later extended the game to spelling other kinds of words, and through it revealed a new grasp of the conventional spellings of short *e* and *o* sounds that was subsequently evident in his writing. He thought "father," which he spelled conventionally, *should* be spelled with an *o*: fother ("father" he pronounces like "n*o*t").

But mainly, during these six months, Paul was interested in activities other than spelling. During his second writing spurt (5:6 through 5:8), he had been working increasingly hard on reading and was moving from reading short bits, like labels on food packages, to reading continuous text in books. Quite early during this second writing period he had demonstrated his ability to read isolated words without context clues (cards in the *Scrabble Alphabet Game*). About the time he wrote his "zig zag zipper book"—during the latter part of this writing period—he sat for a very long time with his *Electric Company Nitty Gritty Rhyming Riddles Book,* trying to figure out every word. Shortly after writing his "report card on sports," Paul was able to play a board game (*Talk and Take*) in which the moves followed directions printed on cards, such as: "Move a triangle to any white space, but do not capture a piece." Reading still clearly involved great effort, but the effort was being rewarded by mastery.

His reading materials at home were no more controlled for repetitive vocabulary or phonic regularity than the language of his writing had been. From the beginning Paul was confronted with all the complexity of English orthography. Since his reading development, like his spelling development, was not based on accumulating memorized sight words, and since he was not receiving any systematic instruction in sound and letter associations beyond "Sesame Street" and "The Electric Company" television programs, he must have been working out some of his own strategies from his observations of regularities. When he asked for help in reading, it was either to confirm the correctness of his reading of a word, or to have the word read for him.

Less than two months after writing his RE.PORT.KARD, Paul read an entire book to me (*Go, Dog, Go!,* a pre-primer story) and then proudly read it to his friend Matthew. He was truly launched into reading. A month later, just before his sixth birthday, he switched to silent reading, reading *Yertle the Turtle* (second grade level) to himself in the car on our way home from the library. By the time he entered first grade (6:1), he had not only taught himself to read, but progressed from laborious decoding to building up speed in reading.

"Once you know how to spell something, you know how to read it," Paul had said when he started inventing spellings. At that point he saw spelling as preceding and enabling reading. But as his reading improved and he became more conscious of conventional spelling, he commented on words he could read but not spell. When he had just started reading silently (6:0), he observed that "hate" was "about the only word I can read but can't spell. I always spell it 'hat.'" Three months later such words seemed more frequent: "Sometimes you can read a word and you can't spell it—like 'dinosaur.' I can read but I can't spell that." "Spelling" now meant to Paul conventional spelling, which he did not see as preceding or enabling reading.

During first grade, there were two strands to Paul's writing, which will be traced separately: the writing he did at school within a broadly specified format, and the writing he did spontaneously at home. Since he was expected to spell conventionally at school and to ask for the spellings of words he needed, which were then written in his own "dictionary," the continuing development of his spelling system must be viewed mainly through his spontaneous writings. His daily school writings, carefully preserved by Paul's first grade teacher, are interesting for their content and for comparisons of concurrent invented and instructed spellings of the same words. These school writings will be considered after we look at his spontaneous productions.

Writings at Home

Evidence of a new visual strategy for spelling, which interfered with his earlier approach of analyzing and representing language sounds, appears in some of Paul's spelling at home during his first two months in first grade (6:2-6:4). Independently he had been spelling "this" and "the" conventionally for some time and representing "th" sounds correctly even longer, yet he wrote TIHS and TEH. He also wrote HUOSE and GOFF (Geoff), a classmate whose name appeared correctly in Paul's "dictionary." Paul had written the *ou* in "house" correctly for months, as he had the *en* in "open," which one day appeared as OPNE. In his classroom the emphasis was on visual spelling, on copying from a correct (adult) model. Paul's errors occurred, it would seem, while he was trying to recall what the words *looked* like. When he was spelling by sound, he had been able to keep letter sequences straight even in three-syllable words. Although his new spelling errors appear to reflect a lack of knowledge about sound-letter relationships and a difficulty with sequencing, his previous writings attest to his competence in these areas. (How might a teacher without this background information on Paul view his errors?) When he used a visual strategy, then, it interfered with his use of a sound strategy.

More mature, competent spellers of English know that a word is correct if it "looks right"; poor, older spellers often try to spell by ear. So although Paul was making errors that he had not made before, they were errors in the direction of progress: in order to master English orthography he would have to remember what words looked like, and when first he focused on that, he temporarily had to abandon his previous and still useful strategy. Biemiller (1970) found a similar learning pattern among beginning readers who first focused on context clues to words, then abandoned context completely as they switched to using sound-letter relationships, but eventually integrated these strategies. Bruner's study (1969) of the integration of sucking and looking in infants also points to an initial interference stage where one activity suppresses the other before succession and finally integration within a larger act is achieved.

Although Paul had earlier grasped the principle that a sound might have alternative spellings, as *K*-A-T and *C*-A-T, he still generally adhered to one spelling for a sound. His greater attention now to the visual aspect of words, not only from his classroom writing but from his reading, was providing him with more information about when alternate spellings were used. The word "closed," which he had always written with a *K,* he now spelled with *C.* He even overgeneralized with *C* in CACE (cake) (6:3), which three months later he spelled CACK, indicating his awareness of a further way to represent the "kuh" sound.

Paul's growing awareness of affixation and his regularization of the spelling of affixes continued to conventionalize his spellings. A sign appeared on a cabinet door: PAUL.S AND MATTHEW.S SAFE. He used the dot again to segment the affix in UN.LOK. A few weeks later this sign was posted inside the bathroom door: THIS IS A SELF LOKING DOOR. In his school "dictionary," where the teacher recorded words Paul requested for writing his stories, Paul had added affixes (indicated here by capitals): lockED, UNlocked, laughING.

Paul started to write more at home during his second month in first grade (6:3), for the most part continuing in his earlier forms: signs and labels, a list, a cookbook, and informative notes telling his whereabouts. One day at the beginning of this quite short period of writing, he imitated the usual form of his school writing: a drawing with a sentence beneath it starting "This is . . . " He asked for the spelling of all the words given in boldface:

THIS. IS. ME. IN. MY. ROOM. **WATCHING. TWO.**
   MICE. GO. INTO. THEIR. HOLE.
THIS. IS. MY. HOUS.
THIS. IS. A. **UPSIDE. DOWN. PICTURE.**

In form, sentence structure, content, and expectation about spelling, his home and school writings seemed worlds apart.

His spontaneous writing then lapsed for a couple of months; when he returned to it during the latter half of first grade, he wrote quite prolifically for five months. One day near the beginning of this period (6:7) he produced four newspapers, which will now be considered closely as indications of his spelling development about ten months after his RE.PORT KARD. and when he had written daily at school, using conventional spellings, for between four and five months. The newspapers were written on large sheets, with the various sections — funnies, weather, news, advertisements — marked off from each other by lines or boxes. Looking over the newspapers three years later, Paul was amazed at his young work: "It's got funnies and advertising and news and weather! How did I get all this? Did I have some interpretation of what was in a newspaper?" He also recalled starting on the project because "I remember Daddy always reading the newspaper, and I thought I'd make one like it." He had, of course, written his *TIMS. R. GIS.* about a year earlier and attempted a newspaper as one of his first writings. That he wrote still another newspaper when he was nine years old attests to his enduring interest in this form, to the possibilities it continued to offer for his inventiveness, sense of humor, and desire to enter into the adult world. (The summary chapter of this section traces Paul's development of the newspaper among other persisting forms in his writing.)

In each of the four newspapers Paul produced that day, FUNE'S (funnies) was the first section, indicating its impor-

tance for him. I would have dismissed this stress as just childish
taste had I not observed Paul's intense interest in book illustrations—especially the details of Richard Scarry's drawings—
during his prereading and early reading years; his love of the
Tintin books, a sophisticated comic-format adventure series,
over a longer span than any other books (from prereading days
when they were read aloud to him up to his present ten years of
age!); the integration of drawing with text in his own writings;
and his absorption, as his drawing skills matured dramatically
during first grade, with detail in his own pictures. The power-
ful appeal of comics, then, seems to lie in its fusion of interesting elements: drawing, language, action, and humor.

Newspaper #1 contained FUNE'S portraying fairly violent
action with little text. Next was an illustrated weather forecast:

THE SAFTERNEWN IT'S GOING TO RAIN.
IT'S GOING TO BE FAIR TOMORO

Then two illustrated advertisements:

BIG SALE! TODAY AT MAKEER'S
GET FISH! AT SEA SCOLAPS

And finally sports news:

1 OF THE BASEBALL TEME'S HIT A HOME RUN
YESTERDAY

The first FUNE in newspaper #2 was titled ON THE
ROAD and showed a car crash, with CRASH written large
and a little stick figure who had escaped, saying "WEW." The
second FUNE was a joke, with one figure asking "WHY DID
YOU PARK THER" and the other replying, "WELL IT
SADE (said) FINE FOR PARKING." There was a headline:
THE ROBER GOT OUT OF JALL (jail) and an ad: GO
SHOPING AT FINEBY.

In newspaper #3 Paul accurately crossed out the 'S in
FUNE'S, leaving FUNE above his single cartoon of a giant
saying "FE FI FO FUM" and a tiny figure crying "HELP!" The
ever-present robbers figured again in the headline: THE
BANGK WAS ROBD.

A news item in paper #4 announced that FAKTARE'S (fac-
tories) CAN NO LONGER OFORD MAKING PLAY DOW

(dough). Drawings of hand tools illustrated an advertisement for TOOL'S! AT HARD WORKER'S. The FUNE'S showed first a motorcycle jump and crash scene titled EVEL KAN-EVEL, and in the second frame, titled LASEE (lazy) LUMPO (a mildly abusive family expression), a person dumping a tray of food on a sleeping person. Both cartoons portrayed in a single picture a sequence of events over time. EVEL KANEVEL was drawn on his cycle heading for the jump, in three positions falling through the air, and finally crashing at the foot of the cliff, saying "OW." LASEE LUMPO was first shown lying down snoring ("ZZ") and then saying "OW" as the food seen on the tray held by the other person is also shown falling upon LASEE.

My first record of Paul's fully working out a time sequence through a series of pictures does not occur until almost two years later. Here he seems to be focusing on the wholeness of the action; later he will differentiate its parts without losing that sense of wholeness. This is one instance among others we shall see here of what Werner describes as "the fundamental law of development — increase of differentiation and hierarchic integration" (1948, p. 44).

The evolution of Paul's invented spelling likewise followed a pattern of increasing differentiation and integration: differentiation of speech sounds to be represented by letters, differentiation of alternative spellings for some sounds; and integration of such information within the framework of systematic conceptions about spelling. Jakobson has described a sequence of stages proceeding "from the simple and undifferentiated to the stratified and differentiated" as the fundamental principle underlying all language development (1968, p. 68). What progress along these lines do we see in Paul's newspaper writings at 6:7, ten months after the last writing we carefully examined, his RE.PORT KARD?

Paul now represents the vowel before syllabic *r* even though it is not heard or felt as a separate sound: AFT*E*R, YEST*E*R, ROB*E*R, WORK*E*R, LONG*E*R. Paul spelled FAIR correctly; a year before this he would have spelled it FAR (like BAR for "bear" and TAR for "there"); less than five months before writing the newspapers, he had spelled it FAER and read "fair"

as "fire." Having taken the step of representing the diphthong-
ization with two vowels, Paul may have assimilated more easily
the conventional spelling (AE to AI). "Fair" was on the list of
words whose spellings he had asked for at school, but he did not
spell all of those same words conventionally when writing at
home.

Paul's representations of the long vowel sounds, for which a
letter name strategy originally sufficed, show a great diversifi-
cation. Where he once only used the letter A, now he uses four
alternative spellings for long *a*:

> *ai* in R*AI*N
> *a* (consonant) *e* in S*A*L*E*, M*A*K*E*, B*A*S*E*
> *ay* in D*AY*, PL*AY*
> and a remnant of the old letter name strategy in J*A*LL (jail)

He also uses four spellings for long *e:*

> *ea* in S*EA*
> *e* (consonant) *e* in T*E*M*E* (team)
> *ee* in LAS*EE* (lazy)
> *e* correctly in B*E* but also in FUN*E* and FAKTAR*E* (funny, fac-
> tory)

While these are all acceptable spellings for the long *e* sound in
English orthography, Paul's choices among alternatives do not
take the position of the sound in the word as much into account
as his long *a* spellings seem to, and he has overlooked *y* as a major alternative for representing the long *e* sound at the end of a
word.

For long *o* he has differentiated four spellings again:

> *oa* in R*OA*D
> *o* (consonant) *e* in H*O*M*E*
> *ow* in D*OW* (dough)
> *o* in G*O*, F*O*, N*O*

Although DOW is incorrect, OW here does not violate environmental constraints (compare mow, grow, low, for example) and is in fact a frequent spelling at the end of a one-syllable
word or stressed syllable.

Paul represents long *i* in three ways:

y in WH*Y*
i (consonant) *e* in F*I*N*E*
i in F*I*

FI is apparently a learned spelling rather than a remnant of letter name strategy, since two weeks before writing this newspaper Paul had written a story in school about a giant in which he had copied FEE, FI, FO, FUM from the adult spelling in his "dictionary." Except for the first person pronoun, the *I* spelling for long *i* does not otherwise appear in his writing.

The long *u* sounds (as in "too" and "cute") are represented by:

oo in T*OO*L
o in D*O*, T*O*
ou in Y*OU*
ew in W*EW* (whew) and N*EW*N (noon, which Paul did not
    diphthongize)

"You" Paul has spelled conventionally for many months, so it probably functions as a learned word rather than a representation of the sounds in a word. Writing his friend Matthew's name many times may be the source of his *ew* spellings.

In becoming aware of these conventional alternatives for representing long vowel sounds, which meant abandoning a simpler system, Paul has taken a big step toward standard orthography. The letter name strategy worked when Paul's apparent goal was to represent speech sounds systematically for himself. His willingness now to deal with the most variable and complex aspect of English orthography means that his goal has clearly shifted to learning conventionally correct spelling.

Although he has differentiated alternative spellings, Paul shows only a partial understanding of the conditions governing the choice of particular alternatives and thus integrating them into a more complex spelling system. (I mean a functional understanding, of course, not necessarily one that can be verbalized.) Six factors conditioning the correspondence between spelling and sound as analyzed by Venezky (1970) and summarized by Gibson and Levin (1975, pp. 179-80) are graphemic environment of the unit, position in the word,

stress, morpheme boundaries, form class, and phonological influences — quite a handful for a six-year-old!

LA*SEE* is an error not in representing the vowel sound per
se but in taking position in the word into account, since *ee* more
commonly represents the long *e* sound in medial rather than
final positions. Paul's spelling of BANGK (bank) — and a few
weeks later STINGKS (stinks) and KANGKER (canker) —
represent a similar error in consonant spellings. Paul does not
yet know that the "ng" sound is spelled *n* rather than *ng* before a
"kuh" sound.

Paul's awareness of morphemes is expanding, as evidenced
in his spelling MAKEER'S (= MAKE + ER + 'S). To
appreciate his development, contrast how he would have
spelled the word a year before: MAKRZ. What he has yet to
learn are the spelling modifications accompanying affixation,
in this case the deletion of an *e*. As is clear from his spelling of
LASEE, he knows that *ee* represents long *e*; thus his morphemic
system overrode his straight phonemics — a further step toward
understanding the principles of English orthography. Weir and
Venezky assert that "if we view this system as a morphophonemic one, more regularity will emerge than will under any
other view" (1973, p. 194). Although in one newspaper Paul
wrote MAKING, this is probably a learned word and one
whose learned spelling can be overcome by his morphemic
sense, since the next week MAKEING appears in a story written at school, and COMEING the following week. He must
have felt sure of these spellings or he would have consulted his
"dictionary" or his teacher.

In Paul's newspapers the dots between words, which persisted after he dropped the dots between syllables or segmenting affixes, have disappeared, and the words are clearly
spaced. He is moving toward conventional punctuation, not
only with the reappearance of his favorite punctuation mark,
the exclamation point, but with the introduction of the
apostrophe, which he overgeneralizes as occurring before the *s*
in plurals as well as possessives and contractions. Twice he uses
the apostrophe correctly in IT'S, which may be something he
learned in school. I note both IT'S and I'M in his school stories
at about this time (6:7), though he most often writes out IT IS

and I AM. The apostrophe for contraction occurs two and a half weeks later in LET'S GO SHOPING TOMARO, and a question mark in another note written to me that same day: MOMY WHEN ARE YOU GOING TO ORDER MY ANAML STAMPS? Three weeks later he used parentheses for the first time: I HAVE GONE TO MATTHEWS (YOU COME DOWN TO PICK ME UP). A week before writing his newspapers, Paul had started using a colon after "to" and "from" (FROM:NOBODY TO:GLENDA). He occasionally closed a sentence with a period, the punctuation mark he received the most instruction about in school; but apparently he found exclamation points, colons, and apostrophes more interesting and significant. At least these were the marks he used most frequently.

During the remainder of Paul's first grade year (6:8-6:11), the spellings in his spontaneous writings show increased sensitivity to position in representing certain long vowel sounds and more frequent use of certain doubled consonants that are common in English orthography. After writing the newspapers, he does not use *E* or *EE* again to represent the long *e* sound in unstressed word-final positions, but *Y* or *EY:* JELLY, HONY, HELLTHY, LABRATOREY. He also drops the *EW* spellings of long *u* in medial positions: K*OO*GL (Koogle), SC*U*P (scoop), an apparent reversion to letter name strategy. Double *t*, which Paul had used earlier only in writing MATTHEW, later appears in PETTER (Peter) and GETTING; double *l* appears in JELLY, HELLTHY, FELL; and double *s*, the first doubled consonant to appear in his spellings outside of proper names (in PASS, almost five months before the newspapers, and again in OFISS and GESS, a few weeks before) continues in TRESPASSING. What is important here is Paul's accepting the principle that both a doubled and a single consonant can represent the same sound. His errors show that he does not understand yet the conditions under which doubling occurs; but without the errors confirming his independent use of consonant doubling, we could not be sure he had accepted this pattern rather than just memorized words containing it.

During this second year of Paul's writing (5:10-6:11) — the first year of his deliberate shift toward conventional spelling and punctuation — we have seen these main developments:

1. Abandonment of his dot segmentation system, followed by a
   time of word spacing but no punctuation, and then increasing use of a variety of conventional punctuation marks.
2. Conventionalization of short vowel representations.
3. Abandonment of the letter name strategy for representing
   long vowel sounds, use of a variety of conventional representations for these sounds, and finally increasing sensitivity to
   conditions determining choices among these alternatives.
4. Operational acceptance of the principle that a single sound,
   which under some conditions is represented by a single letter, under different conditions may be represented by two
   letters: ER for syllabic *r,* and doubled consonants.
5. Use of a new visual recall strategy for spelling.
6. Extended awareness of affixes and the regularization of their
   spellings in spite of some phonemic differences.

In short, Paul's original tacit conception of spelling as a
phonemic transcription of speech sounds has been transformed
into a more complex system, closer to the nature of English orthography. The interference effect produced at first by his
visual recall strategy has disappeared, signifying the integration of this strategy with phonemic and morphemic strategies —
an integration that could only take place within the broader
framework of a more complex conception of spelling.

The sources of Paul's information about spelling during this
second year were more diverse and their influence difficult to
assess. He selected from his school instruction (the words written correctly for him and the spelling patterns in the workbooks), from responses to the questions he asked about spelling
at home, and from his considerable reading, which included
reading from the television screen. He told me he had learned
to spell "walk" from seeing it on "Sesame Street"; he also spelled
DI-GEL and ALKASELTSER [*sic*]. After reviewing the development of the forms of his writing during this year, we will look
at his school writings and compare them, in forms and spellings, with his spontaneous writings at home.

During this year Paul continued to write in all of the forms he
had used the year before as an inventive speller: signs and labels,
books, directions, newspapers, notes, stories, games, lists. He
also started writing in some new forms: rhymes, riddles, and a
personal notebook which much later evolved into a diary.

Signs and labels, integrating writing with play activities and with drawing, were his most frequent forms. In the middle of this year (6:6) he drew shelves on which were set containers of varying shapes labeled JAM, JELLY, HONY, PICKLS, HELLTHY (healthy), KOOGL CINAMIN, DI-GEL NEW LMN ORING, DONUTS, DI-GEL MINT, KECHUP, ALKASELTSER, MUSTRD, SALT, PEPER, PUFS, and KANGKER SOR.STUF (figure 2). Paul also had a SIHN (sign) STORE for which he made these signs:

FARMERS MARKIT	DO NOT DESTERB
WET PAINT	RESTERANT
LABRATOREY	ROBOT HERE
SHH!	CLOSED
NO TRESPASSING	OPEN

Not all of his signs were imitations of signs from the adult world. Two months earlier he had produced this series:

GO AWAY	NEVER MIND
LEVE ME ALON	GET OUT
GET LOST	BUG OFF
DON'T BOTER ME	

In the light of Paul's interest in writing signs and labels (an interest that continues in the years ahead), it seems no accident or mere effect of brevity that signs and labels were his main beginning reading materials.

The second most frequent form of writing Paul used when he was six years old was notes, including informative notes, personal notes, and greeting cards. The informative notes were mostly to tell me where he had gone after school (he got home a little earlier than I did): IM.OUT.4.A.WALK. IL.BE.BAK (originally BAKE, but Paul crossed out the *E*), written very early that year; and six months later, I HAVE GONE TO MATTHEWS (YOU COME DOWN TO PICK ME UP). He also wrote a reminder to himself about a television program he wanted to see: SUNEAY (Sunday—I cannot explain that *E*) CHANEL 3730 FROSTEI THE SNOW MAN, written mid-year. Birthday cards and valentines continued: WHEN YOU ARE ARAWND MY HAR 'OWVER' (over—to other side of paper) JUMPS GESS WHO. Occasionally writing forms prac-

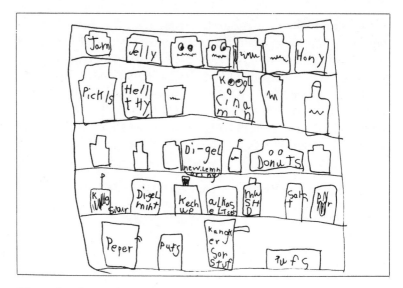

Figure 2. *Shelves of containers (6:7).*

ticed in school appeared in his spontaneous writings at home, one being the formally addressed envelope in which some of his notes were delivered. Two notes "in cursive," according to Paul—that is, rows of wavy lines—were the closest he came to the scribble writing which in some children's development precedes writing with letters.

The first book he wrote at the beginning of this year was an illustrated pop-up book—a kind of book he especially enjoyed reading—which he was proud of because "you can learn something from it." The book contained:

I am not sure whether the "something" to be learned was reading or concepts, but the book recalls Paul's earlier "writing class" showing how to spell a list of words, and conveys his youthful appreciation of reading in order to learn. (The fact that his parents were teachers may not be irrelevant here.) He also wrote several COOK BOOKs, listing foods such as GRAPS,

CARETS, STRABARES, LETES, PIE, POTATO, BRED, CHERES, CACK; and a tiny CODE BOOK with symbols he had devised for twelve letters.

Paul's teacher encouraged her first graders to make books, so there was more overlap here between home and school writings than in any other form; Paul would sometimes finish at home a book he had started at school, and on at least one occasion he wrote a book independently at school. His original contribution to MY BOOK, started as a school project, was a table of contents on the front cover called WHAT'S INSIDE, giving in order the text of each illustrated sentence and its page number, such as THIS.IS.A.CHAIR 4. We see again his interest in the formal aspects of books, as in the dedication "for Juan" several months earlier. As a reader, he made good use of indexes and tables of contents.

The day Paul got his first grade midyear report card (age 6:6), he made report cards for our dog and three cats which were "report cards" in the school sense of evaluation rather than in the sense of a news "report," like his earlier "report card on sports." The categories were PEING (peeing—we had a male cat problem), HOME WORK, ABSINT, and REDING (reading); the marks were GOOD and 0 (zero).

He wrote only one story in the traditional story form he had used twice the year before, but this time the "story" was all form and no content: ONECS UPON A TIME THERE WAS A CAT. THE END (6:10). Some of the sentences he wrote under his drawings at school were more truly stories involving plot, such as: "This is the police chasing me and I am going to go up a ramp and I am going to land in a hole and the hole is my hide out" (6:7).

Paul continued to write instructions, including a recipe for "dump cookies," his version of drop cookies (6:8):

INGREDEINS
2 CUP'S OF FLOUR
1 CUP OF HONY
1 EGG
1 SCUP (scoop) OF BUTER
WHAT TO DO.
BEET UP WITH BETER

His headings INGREDEINS and WHAT TO DO again indicate his awareness of the formal structure of written material
and also of categorization, which fascinates him the year after
this.

The games he devised as a six-year-old were more verbal
and academic than the previous year's board game, including
an alphabet with two missing letters to fill in, and a word-
building grid:

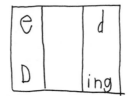

While continuing to write in all these and other forms he had
used as a five-year-old, Paul added some new ones: rhymes,
riddles, and a personal notebook (eventually a diary). He was
not conscious of the conventional line arrangement of rhymed
verse, which he had read very little when he wrote this verse
(6:9):

PETTER (Peter) — PETTER —
PETTER PART
HIS BIG OLD
PUMKIN FELL
APART HE TRYED
TO STOP IT
WITH A DART PETTER — — —
The dashes at the end indicate a repeat, since Paul had run out
of room at the bottom of the page.

As a six- and seven-year-old Paul was intrigued with riddles.
The second book Paul read entirely at one sitting as a five-year-
old was his "Electric Company" *Nitty Gritty Rhyming Riddles
Book,* which he worked long and hard on reading. His
heightened interest in arithmetic and large numbers when he
had just turned six was expressed in this spoken riddle: "How
many steps would it take a giant to walk around the universe?"
Six months later he made up a "silly science riddle": "What
once was a rock but without the ocean it wouldn't be smaller
than you are? What is it? Sand." And this one: "People are on it

and you can't take them off and they never go inside. What is it? A TV." He also wrote riddles, sometimes joke-type riddles he had heard, and sometimes another riddle he had made up, like this one (6:7):

I AM AWACK (awake) AT NITE ASLEP IN THE DAY
BUT I AM NOT A OWL

ANSER ON OTHER SIDE

THE MOON

As we trace the forms of Paul's writing over five years, they become more themes than forms, merging with his reading interests and his activities, expressing his style as a learner and his concerns as a person.

When he was almost seven, Paul wrote in the notebook he kept in his room:

SOME TIMS I HATE SCOLL (school)
I HATE GETTING MY WORK RONG
I HATE GETTING IN TRUBLE
I HATE LOSEING MARBLE GAMES

He later shared this writing with me, but it was not written *for* me. In this expression of his feelings, and in the note written to remind himself to watch a television program, we see the beginnings of Paul's writing for himself as audience, as his sense of self and separateness develops.

Writings at School

In contrast to the varied forms of Paul's spontaneous writings, his school writings were structurally monotonous. The basic daily writing format was the picture-story done on large sheets of paper, blank at the top for drawing a picture and ruled at the bottom for writing something about the picture. Phrases like "This is," which could be used to start stories, were available on cards for children who wanted to copy them; but the teacher made no restriction on the forms of the stories. Nevertheless, almost all of Paul's stories during the entire year started out "This is . . ." As an eight-year-old reading over some of these first grade stories, Paul himself wondered aloud why he kept repeating statements. Repetition was not characteristic of his spontaneous writings.

But in school Paul wrote for a different purpose and a different audience and in the context of different expectations for his writing than at home. Not only was conventional spelling expected — which was in accord with Paul's changed though less rigorously enforced expectations for himself — but also proper letter formation, spacing, and writing on the line. At home, Paul wrote using a combination of uppercase and lowercase letter forms, with an increasing proportion becoming lowercase; he was using dots rather than spaces between words when he entered first grade; his handwriting was not neat; and he hardly ever wrote on lined paper. He tended to arrange sentences so they had their own space on a page or were enclosed in boxes. Aside from my comment about spacing soon after Paul started writing, I had simply not been concerned about the appearance of his writing. He had expressed pride once the year before in being able to write small letters, but otherwise seemed to focus on working out his spellings.

At school, he was not expected to figure out spellings but to copy them and eventually learn words by repeatedly writing them. During the first weeks of school, he brought home slips of paper with words he had requested for writing his stories, each word copied over four times beneath the teacher's model. Paul's words were "cross," "tree," "chair," "far," "dog," "TV," and "no." At least the last three were words he obviously knew. When I asked him why he had wanted "dog," one of his first conventional spellings, written for him, he said because he didn't want a word with a lot of letters he didn't know how to make. At this time the first graders were working on penmanship, practicing a few lowercase letters every day. Although the teacher told me she was not concerned about penmanship in the stories, Paul was. As was evident in his early letter writing, he was more self-conscious about his writing when people outside his immediate family would be reading it. At the begining of the year, when a story Paul had dictated was written under his picture, Paul traced over the teacher's writing rather than copying it on the line below as assigned. Since he already knew how to write, what could he see as the point except to learn how

to write differently? There were other times in school, beyond
first grade, when Paul misunderstood an assignment because
what was required seemed to him too simple and obvious to be
right.

Another difference from writing at home was the audience in
school — perhaps the other children more than the teacher.
How important was it to Paul to write as they did? Instead of
writing by himself, he was writing in a group. Instead of
writing when he had something in particular he wanted to
write, he wrote during class writing periods.

When I initially looked over Paul's first grade stories, I was
disappointed by a repetitiousness which had not characterized
his writings at home. Here is a random sampling of his stories:

> This is me getting hurt (6:3)
> This is my house on the Hill (6:4)
> This is my gun (6:5)
> Paul B. doesnt like ramming into a rock (6:6)
> I was runing and somebody shot me when I was runing. I am
>   dead now (6:7)
> This is me eating a pickle (6:8)
> These are the clubs marbles (6:9)
> This is my reading book (6:10)

However, returning to study his stories later, I began to see
how Paul's creative energy was often channeled to the drawings
rather than the text, as in his early story, "This.is.pollution"
(figure 3). At the center of the picture rises a tall building belch-
ing smoke from four chimneys; to the left of it are two figures
smoking, one a pipe and the other a cigarette, under a dark
cloud; to the right of the building, under another smoke cloud,
are two figures coughing.

I also came to see, in the perspective of Paul's later development, themes and stylistic characteristics emerging from these
stories and drawings, whose content was not so impoverished
as I had first thought. Paul has always enjoyed constructing
and inventing things since he was old enough to do so. Several
of his picture-stories describe devices such as that by which an
airplane lifts a giant's arm (figure 4). A blend of fantasy and
realism tinged with humor — a style characterizing stories Paul
was to write in third grade — is already evident in his story,

Figure 3.   *"This is Pollution" (6:3).*

"This is Samantha and her seven is magic workbook and she is makeing me disappear." (*Seven Is Magic* is the title of the reading text some of the first graders were using.) Paul's careful attention to details, which also characterizes his much later writings, can be seen now in his drawings. Thus his stories, though constrained in form, were still expressive.

Paul's spellings in his writings at school were almost always correct: that was the expectation, the teacher was there to provide correct models, and words were repeated more frequently in Paul's school than his home writings. It is easier to discern which of these correct spellings did not carry over into his spontaneous writing than to be sure which correct spellings or spelling principles were learned from his school story writing. As is ever the case in classrooms, what was taught was not identical with what was learned. Children's learning is sometimes less, sometimes more, and sometimes other than the explicit instruction. Paul had written, for example, "because" and "might" correctly in a school story, but about a month later he independently spelled these same words BECOS and MIHT.

When such differences occur we can ask what it is about the

Figure 4. *"Airplane lifting a Giant's arm" (6:8).*

spellings that may have made them difficult for Paul to assimilate into his system, thus possibly illuminating some of the structures in that system. However, since Paul's writing vocabularies at home and school overlapped very little, there are too few examples of common words spelled divergently to confirm definite patterns. MIHT shows some visual recall and awareness of a silent consonant, which he may even have generalized: about two months later he wrote SIHN (sign) and almost a year later, RIHT (right). He *read* words like "night" and "light" without difficulty, and just before setting up his SIHN STOR, he had been reading at school a book called *Mr. Pine's Mixed Up Signs.* Paul's strong sense of meaning and his use of context probably enabled him to overcome the decoding problems in such words. "Because" is a word he rarely uses in writing although it is frequent in his speech (which suggests that he is not yet using written language for exploring causality). Surely he must have seen "because" many times in print before writing BECOS. Although the *au* pattern exists in his name, it does not appear in his spellings until the middle of the second grade, after he has mastered the phonemically more inexplicable *gh* pattern: CAGHT (caught), TOGHT (taught),

LAGHED (laughed) at 7:5; then DINSOU*A U*R and TYR-RANAS*A U*RYS at 7:6.

On the other hand, "marbles" — a word Paul used frequently in his school stories during the spring marble season when he was an avid player — later appears correctly in his independent writing (I HATE LOSEING MARBLE GAMES), and the *ble* may have generalized to the spelling of TRUBLE in the same piece. Up to that point he generally did not represent a vowel with syllabic *l* (LITTL, PICKL, KOOGL, MARVL), but when he did, he had placed it *before* the *l* (MARVIL, KANEVEL). Since Paul had already accepted "silent e," this pattern could be easily assimilated.

Generalizing spelling patterns and principles from an unstructured set of correctly spelled words and accumulating learned words was the way Paul had been learning anyway. In first grade he also received explicit workbook instruction in spelling patterns (Stern, *We Read and Write,* grade level 1²). Most of the patterns Paul already used correctly in his spontaneous writings: final blends like *-st, -nd,* and *-sh;* initial blends like *dr-, sl-,* and *sp-.* As mentioned earlier, the workbook contained several exercises on the vowel + *nk* pattern, which Paul did correctly in the book (except for a *g* he then crossed out in "pingk"), yet during the latter half of first grade, after doing the workbook, he wrote independently BANGK, KANGKER and STINGKS. In the exercises on the vowel + *ck* pattern, he occasionally used a *k* instead of *ck,* and he seemed to have trouble generalizing this spelling correctly in his independent writing, as in his spellings of CACK (cake) and AWACK (awake). (He was only beginning to be aware of the effect of letter environment on sound-spelling relationships at this time.) The summer after first grade, he wrote GOOD LUK.

There were some workbook words with double *l* and a few with double *s,* which may have contributed to establishing those patterns in Paul's independent spelling: JALL (jail), SCOLL (school), GESS (guess). The workbook included much practice on short vowel spellings, which Paul had largely mastered before entering first grade. In sum, he learned little about spelling from this workbook. A more advanced one that included polysyllabic and Latinate words could have provided richer material for him. But his teacher did not have his independent writings before her, as I did, to assess his spelling needs; and she had to instruct twenty-some other children, most of whom had greater literacy-learning needs than Paul.

How much do the changes seen in Paul's spelling and writing during this year (as summarized on pages 51 to 52) seem to have been affected by first grade instruction?

1. Abandonment of his dot segmentation system in favor of conventional spacing and punctuation marks. This most likely resulted from classroom writing, although some punctuation marks were independently acquired. Other matters of appearance — standard letter formations, conventional use of lowercase letters and capitalization, writing on lines — were at least hastened by classroom expectations. It is my sense that Paul's own concern with correctness would have led him to conform to these standards in time. (He writes with his left hand, which may have slowed his handwriting development.)

2. Conventionalization of short vowel representations. These had been largely achieved during several months before first grade.

3. Changes in long vowel representation. Paul's abandonment of letter name strategy, use of alternative representations, and increasing responsiveness of conditions governing the choice among alternatives are difficult to trace to any particular source. He received no explicit instruction in these patterns (except for a brief workbook exercise on $a-e$), so his learning was independent. Certainly his school story writing provided words from which he could have drawn such generalizations.

4. Operational acceptance of the principle that a single sound, which under some conditions may be represented by a single letter, under different conditions may be represented by two letters (syllabic r and doubled consonants). This could have been drawn from his school writings among other sources.

5. Use of a new visual strategy for spelling. Although this was beginning to show in Paul's writing before first grade, school certainly strengthened it.

6. Extended awareness of affixes and the regularization of their spellings in spite of some phonemic differences. Paul did not receive instruction here, though again his first grade

writings provided materials he could have drawn his own
generalizations from.

For the most part, then, the generalizations about spelling
came from Paul. Materials from which to draw those generalizations were around him at school and at home. Certainly the
daily story writing in first grade made spelling materials abun-
dantly available to him. It is hard to know how Paul's spelling
development might have been different without all that classroom writing, but we will see how it goes in second grade when
he did only workbook writing in school. As a six-year-old he
read a lot, so books were another source of spelling materials.

What is interesting is the way Paul *selects* from the material
around him. Jakobson (1968) has shown how infants select the
speech sounds they produce from a rich phonemic environment
according to the principle of phonemic opposition (starting
with the most fundamental, vowel-consonant distinction) and
construct a phonemic system through a universal sequence of
distinctions and stratifications, building from the foundation
up. Read (1971), who has observed through children's invented
spelling some of the ways preschoolers categorize and alpha-
betically represent English speech sounds, sees some children
entering school with a foundation in the alphabetic principle
of English spelling. Subsequently, the child's task is not to
memorize long lists of words or to be trained in correct spelling
"habits," but "to master new principles that extend and deepen
the already abstract conception of the sound system of English
that he brings to school" (Read, 1971, p. 13).

The first two years of Paul's spelling development document
this point of view.

7:0-7:11 (Second Grade)

During the summer between first and second grades, the
summer of Paul's seventh birthday, he wrote very little. In the
fall our family moved to the city for the academic year, and
new friends, bike riding, making and spending money, inventing, and working with numbers were Paul's main interests for
some time. Soon after school opened, he announced that he
hated writing, but I am not sure what "writing" he referred to.
In school about the only writing he did was in workbook exer-

cises and spelling lists. At home, until mid-November, he still wrote very little: signs, labels, notes—a few of his old basic forms.

But old forms were coming to serve new purposes: he was using writing to remember, keep track of, and organize things. He made a book (7:2) called PAULS COLECSHINS, tabulating his possessions: SPOONS 37, PETS 2, COMICS 4, MARBLES 4, MONY 2$, MAGIC ECT 3. (The ECT matched his pronunciation of "ectcetera.") On each page, below the label, was a sort of grid for recording the numbers; on the MONY page was a column for $ and one for ¢. This book accompanied a strong interest in sorting—his toy cars, Halloween candies, football player cards—and re-sorting according to different categories; for example, the football player cards were sorted first by teams, then by color features on the card. He laid out his schoolwork in chart form (7:3) with a square for each kind: SPELING, SPESHEL PROJECTS, M (math), RW (*Rewards* workbook), RR (*Rewards* reading), MAD LIBS, and the reward for all the work in the final column, CANDY. While he continued to leave notes telling where he had gone after school, he also started to write notes explicitly to himself: PAUL DONT FORGET (7:3). He also extended his imitations of adult forms to "licenses" and "college ID's" for his toy animals, drawn in fill-in chart form with squares for such information as AGE, NAME, GRADE, ADRESS, ONER or OWNER. A final new aspect to his writing that appeared before his big writing spurt of this year was invented names—something he continued the next year. These were imaginary street names, pronounced as you would expect except where indicated: GONG (jong), GOOP, FOP, COKEY (cocky), FINGY (7:4).

What led Paul back to more writing again? But wait— behind that question seems to lie an assumption that learning, interests, activities continue at constant rates. Anyone who has observed children or observed his own life patterns knows their inevitable flux. Curriculum materials, traditional school schedules, and standardized tests convey a false sense of learning as a steady-rate process. In looking at individual children, we see the ebb and flow of their interests, of the activities they engage in most wholeheartedly, and consequently of much of their learning. That Paul had recurring writing spurts and reading spurts bespeaks his spontaneous involvement with these activities rather than routine accomplishment of daily bite-sized portions. Still, understanding the conditions of these spurts might help us understand Paul's purposes for writing (and reading).

Paul's writing spurt for the year, which lasted about two months (7:4-7:7), coincided with the period when I was writing up the first year of this research and often had Paul's five-year-old writings spread out on my desk. Just before Thanksgiving he had been interested in looking them over and persisted in trying to read them, even though he was now so far removed from his invented spelling system that it was difficult for him. The omission of preconsonantal nasals (for example, WAT for "went") and the use of final *E* to represent the long vowel sound (for example, ANE for "any") gave him the most trouble. "This is like a secret code book," he said, dramatizing how his writing had changed in two years.

These early writings and my absorption in them may have stimulated him to write again; and the holidays provided occasions for writing at home. On Thanksgiving day (7:4) he made out a schedule for himself:

PAUL PLEASE DO THIS
1 MAKE BASSKITS ETC
2 ORGANISE
3 TV
4 FIND OUT WHAT JOE FROGERS ARE
5 EAT

A week later (7:4) he wrote up a sheet of TRAIN RULES for his electric train (reproduced in figure 5):

UNPLUG WHEN DONE USING TRAIN
TRAIN **SHOULD** BE UNPLUGED WHEN IT NEDS
   REPIAR
GREEN ON
RED OFF
TRACK SHOUD BE STRAIT WHEN OTAMATIK CUO-
   PLE
IF YOU WANT TO MAKE THE TRAIN GO FAST MAKE
   THE RI**GH**T TRACK

Figure 5. *"Train Rules" (7:4).*

This information was for others using his train, but Paul also seemed to enjoy the codifying process and the tangible representation of his "rules," which were hung on the wall. That is, though the audience for this writing was ostensibly others and its intent to inform, Paul at the same time was his own audience, enjoying the power of organizing and publishing his "rules."

As is evident in figure 5, he had several struggles with spelling. The worst was over the word "should" which, probably from visual recall, he knew contained an *L;* but wherever he put it (SHLOLD, SHOLD, SLHOD), it did not look right. He could neither hear nor reason its position, so he finally

asked me how to spell "should." The next time he spelled the
word (TRACK SHOUD BE STRAIT), he remembered the *U*
but dropped the troublesome *L*. Other evidence of visual spellings is seen in his attempt to correct RIT by changing it to
RIHT. When that did not satisfy him, he asked me, and
spelled it correctly when I told him it was spelled like "light"
and "night." CUOPLE also indicates visual recall; it certainly
is not a phonetic spelling. Although his spellings often show
good recall of vowel combinations, he is not yet sure of the
order of the vowels; thus he writes SHOUD but CUOPLE,
and STRAIT and TRAIN but REPIAR. His ear is better than
his visual memory for spelling, and phonemic spellings like
OTAMATIK (automatic) still appear, though less frequently
now. NEDS (needs) seems anachronistic here, but he also initially spelled "green" with one *E* and then corrected it. Evidence
of a spelling rule, probably from school instruction, is his crossing out the *E* from USEING.

Clearly Paul is using multiple spelling strategies now:
phonemic, visual, and perhaps even rule-guided. Although
visual recall does not always enable him to spell words correctly, it seems crucial to his detection of errors: he sees that words
do not look right and then tries to correct them. It is hard to
know whether he thought OTAMATIK was correct or
rather—as I suspect was the case—knew he could not spell it
and so settled for a satisfactory phonemic representation.

"You know what? I'm getting to like writing now," he said
while working on PAUL'S SONG AND RIME BOOK (7:5).
He started writing this book while I was playing Christmas
carols; it contained three original Christmas lyrics as well as
three verses on other themes such as:

    WE KILLED, THE BRITISH. (title)
    WE KILLED THE BRITISH
    AND THEY ALL DIED
    WE KILLED THE BRITISH
    AND WE SURVIVED
    WE ALWAYS FAGHT OUR
    BATELS TRUE
    AND THAT IS ALWAYS
    TOLD TO YOU.

The rhyming words occurring at the end of lines may be a function of the paper size, since this arrangement did not hold for most rhymes in the other verses. Paul never returned to such intensive rhyme-writing during the period of this study, although he made up oral rhymes and read and reread Shel Silverstein's book of verse *Where the Sidewalk Ends.*

The *gh* combination that gave Paul trouble in RIHT eleven days ago is now correct in FAGHT and continues to be correct in TOGHT (taught), LAGHED (laughed), CAGHT (caught) and LIGHT, all written within the following month. Three months later he was working on words with *gh* for his spelling lessons at school and of course had no trouble spelling them correctly (for example, through, brought, right).

Despite its occurrence in his first name, *au* was one of the later vowel combinations Paul learned—and not through an absence of instruction or practice. In first grade, "because" and "laugh" were written in his dictionary (independently he wrote BECOS), and he wrote ASTRONAUT in a book report he did at school. Beyond the double vowels OO and EE used at five years, the first conventional vowel combination he used was EA with the letters invariably in proper sequence: SEA (6:7), DEAD and SNEAKERS (7:4). The only occurrence of AE was during his invented spelling period when he sounded out "fair" (diphthongized in his prounication): FAER (5:11). Some other vowel combinations representing single sounds (that is, not diphthongs) seemed to be treated as units, with at least occasional reversals of sequence: ABSALOUTLY (7:5), HILAROUS (7:6), but CUOPLE (7:4) and SCHRUMP-SHUOS (7:7); TRAIN and STRAIT, but REPIAR (7:4). The IE combination, which occurs more frequently in that order in English orthography, Paul more often wrote EI: FROSTEI (Frosty, 6:4), REICIPIE (7:5), SIREIS (series, 7:6), ENCYCLOPEIDA (7:10).

Paul's learning of conventional vowel combinations did not seem to have been primarily influenced by the frequency of their occurrence. He learned OI relatively early: NOIS (6:6), TOILET (7:5); and OE: FOE, MEMOES (plural of MEMO, both at 7:4). In fact OI was so well established, although infrequently reinforced in writing or reading, that it appeared to interfere with his learning the *-tion* ending for a whole year after he discovered it was not spelled SHUN or SHIN or SHON: COLECSHINS (7:2), COLECTOIN and IDENTAFACAI-TOIN (7:5), EXAMANATOIN (7:9), DIRECTIONS (8:1, but he was unsure whether it was IO or OI until 8:5). The fact that Paul had been given and used in his first grade school stories the spellings of POLLUTION, SUCTION, and IN-VENTION had no effect on his spelling of words ending in *-tion*. Such words did not appear on his school spelling lists until after he had mastered the spelling on his own.

Clearly, at least in the instances described here, neither instruction, practice, nor frequency of occurrence in print was directly related to Paul's learning about spellings. Yet equally clearly, letter sequences unacceptable in English orthography (for example, the AOO in HAOOS, house, 5:2) were disappearing from his writing, and the misspelled words he wrote as a seven-year-old looked more like English. While he was, to be sure, accumulating a store of correctly spelled individual words, more importantly he was tacitly learning the rules of English orthography that differed from his "rules" for invented spelling. Only rule-type learning of a kind beyond his school instruction could account for the number of words he spelled conventionally as well as for the nature of his misspellings. He had not concluded that English orthography was too unpredictable to understand.

The main sources of his spelling "instruction" at this point I judge to be his reading (which was fairly extensive both in and out of school) coupled with his writing, his interest in words, and his continuing responsibility for and direction of his own learning.

Most of the time Paul tried to figure out spellings on his own, but occasionally he asked for the spelling of a word, such as "combination." During the earlier part of the year, although his questions were in the form of "How do you spell ———?" he did not need the entire spelling but enough to solve a problem with a particular part of the word. After asking how to spell "merry," he said, "I just wanted to know if it had one or two *r*'s" (7:4). Later in the year the form of his questions sounded more like an adult's as he made the particular problem explicit: "Do you spell 'hoping' with two *p*'s?" or "Do you spell 'page' p-a-g-e or p-a-d-g-e?" (7:7). He was intrigued with different ways of representing a word and compiled a list (including suggestions from his parents) of twenty-six ways to spell "off." Although he got a dictionary during this year, he used it more to explore word meanings than to look up spellings. After writing it, he sometimes asked if he had spelled a word correctly, like "identification" and "dinosaur."

He challenged himself to spell words more difficult than many on his weekly school lists:

    I WILL TYPE SOME WORDS (7:6)
    RYDICKYOLIS   ACOMPLISH
    DINSOUAUR

and the next day:

    I WILL TYPE SOME WORDS
    TYRANNASAURYS REX   LAHGFING
    GARBAGE   HILAROUS   NOGGIN
    TELEFONE   INDAN   TYPERITER

Four months later (7:10) he asked me to give him some hard spelling words and wrote:

    EXERCISE   MASSACHUSETTS
    ENCYCLOPEIDA   EXPLOSIVES
    PHYSISHUN   WORCHESTER
    DINOSOUR   SYMPHONY
    ASTRONOT

A challenge is something that will stretch your powers, with the likelihood of confirming them; you want to take on a challenge because you have confidence enough that you can succeed. A threat is a task that seems beyond your powers to accomplish or cope with. In setting his own tasks, Paul was able to keep them at the challenge level. He was not content to repeat his accomplishments but spontaneously moved on to harder tasks, as I had observed him do as a five-year-old playing in the water. While in an inner tube, he first just ducked his head under water, then ducked it and came up outside the tube, and when he had mastered that, ducked outside the tube and came up inside it. He set up a progression of increasingly difficult tasks for himself as many other children spontaneously do. How much might self-set challenges occur in school learning if time and space were allowed for them to happen and to be observed?

Success through persistence is the theme of a story Paul wrote near the end of this writing spurt (7:6):

> ONCE APON A TIME THERE WAS A LITTLE RABIT
> HOW HAD NO HOME
> SO HE LOOKED FOR ONE IN THE DISTANCE HE
> COULD SEE A LIGHT HE WENT TOWARD IT
> IT WAS A HOUSE AT LAST HE HAD A HOME!!
> HE WENT IN THIS IS WHAT IT LOOKED LIKE
> (drawing of the interior)
> THEN A MAN CAME OUT OF A DOOR AND TOOK
> THE RABIT OUT
> THE RABIT CAME BACK TO THE HOUSE THIS
> TIME THE MAN FELT SORRY FOR THE RABIT
> AND LET THE RABIT IN AND THE RABIT AND
> THE MAN LIVED HAPPLY EVER AFTER   THE
> END

Many of the forms Paul wrote in as a seven-year-old have already been mentioned here: signs, labels, notes, charts and organizers, lists, rhymes and stories, and imitations of adult functional forms like licenses. Except for the charts and organizers (for example, schedules), these are developments of forms he had used earlier; so were the newspaper, fun book, directions, and school-type exercises (punctuation worksheets) he also wrote during this year. The continuity of forms over these three years of Paul's writing is striking, though perhaps not surprising since he started out with such a varied repertoire.

This continuity of forms, however, is not mere repetition; the contents, as in his stories, become extended and elaborated, and forms such as signs assume new functions. NO PARKING ANY TIME and LOOK BOTH WAYS BEFORE CROSSING STRET (7:5) bring the adult world into the world of Paul's play, whereas PAULZ RABR SAF RABRZ KANT GT EN (Paul's robber safe. Robbers can't get in. 5:6) imposed his world upon adult forms—in this case a kitchen cabinet. Assimilation of the adult world to his own and accommodation of his world to that of adults have both been evident in his writings all along. Writing was an important avenue for these transactions and thus not only reflected Paul's growing up but was part of that process. Through writing he came to use and understand adult reality and to make some of it his own. This should be reflected on in planning school writing programs for young children; such programs now often focus only on stories, short answers to workbook questions, and an occasional poem.

The continued conventionalizing of Paul's writing — and his world — is evident as his seven-year-old writings can more easily be classified in traditional categories such as "creative" and "functional." He no longer writes factual material in story ("once upon a time") form, nor fantasy in factual forms. His sense of audience is more differentiated and clearly implied — a conventionalization as well as a maturation. Much of Paul's writing even at the beginning distinguished written from spoken forms, and as a seven-year-old his writing continued to be very much influenced by the adult written forms he saw around him at home (newspapers, books, notes, and so on), at school (report cards, workbooks), and in the world at large (signs, directions). Except in his rhymes and stories, he writes most of the time as a participant rather than as a spectator, in James Britton's terms (1970a) — to interact with people and things, to make things happen rather than to contemplate what has happened or might happen.

In the next section we will see how Paul as an eight-year-old extends his spectator role both by employing new forms of writing (diary and observational recording) and refining old ones (notably the story). We will also see that his mastery of many principles and facts of English spelling (especially through his awareness of less common, more Latinate morphemes) leaves him yet to learn only infrequent distinctions and relatively minor facts.

4 Paul: Sustained and More Mature Writing

8:0-9:8 (Third and Fourth Grades)

In contrast to previous years, much of Paul's most interesting writing was done or initiated at school during third grade. The flowering of Paul's school writing reflects not only his own growth as a writer but the kinds of assignments and responses he received from an imaginative, flexible, and warmly supportive teacher. Although he was surely no less competent a writer in fourth grade, his school writings tended to be more routine and shorter.

After the third graders had read a story about a magic go-cart, the teacher asked them to write a story about a magic go-cart or carpet, which they were given a week to complete. That time was important for Paul (I think he took even longer, writing both at school and at home), who is not a fast writer and often did not finish written work within short time limits.

Paul's story integrates many of his earlier writing interests — detailed illustrations that include labels ("I like labeling stuff," he remarked to me in discussing the story later), rhymes, a story line, and an interest in complicated causation as seen earlier in his drawings and constructions of machines but now in plot development. He bound the story as a book and included the formalities of an index of chapter and page numbers, author credits and, on the book cover, a photograph of "the author of this book." His drawings show his usual interest in detail, but that interest is now also expressed through his writing in descriptive details like "then it [the magic carpet] started going what seemed like 100 miles per hour." A page from the story is reproduced in figure 6.

As a story writer—and this was the third story Paul wrote during the first months of third grade—he has discovered dialogue and description, in contrast to his earlier bare narratives of events. He has also developed an acute sense of audience, evident from the very beginning when he explains who the characters are ("two of my best friends" and "Kenny's sister") rather than assuming that the reader knows Kenny, Matthew, and Robin, as he would have when he was younger. The egocentrism of young children makes taking another point of view into account difficult or impossible. Connie and Harold Rosen note that six- and seven-year-olds assume the reader's interest and knowledge, and that at times they "talk to themselves on the page." "When once the writer becomes aware that he must take active steps to accommodate the reader," they observe, "his writing will change in certain important respects" (Rosen and Rosen, 1973, p. 137). At one point Paul even interrupts the story to address the audience directly: "I suppose you want to know how you steer a magic carpet . . ." This audience awareness is perhaps the most dramatic change of all in his story writing and helps to account for the details, dialogue, and careful explanations which make this and other stories real to the reader as well as to the writer. In his accounting for all events and his realistic detail—assuming the single extravagance of the magic carpet—he attends to credibility and presents us (as poet Marianne Moore said) an imaginary garden with real toads in it. The central themes of power and control run through other stories he wrote this year, reflecting not only the dreams but the tensions of growing up.

A Magic Carpet or Two (8:4)
story by Paul Bissex
pictures by Paul Bissex
whole book by Paul Bissex
Chapter I

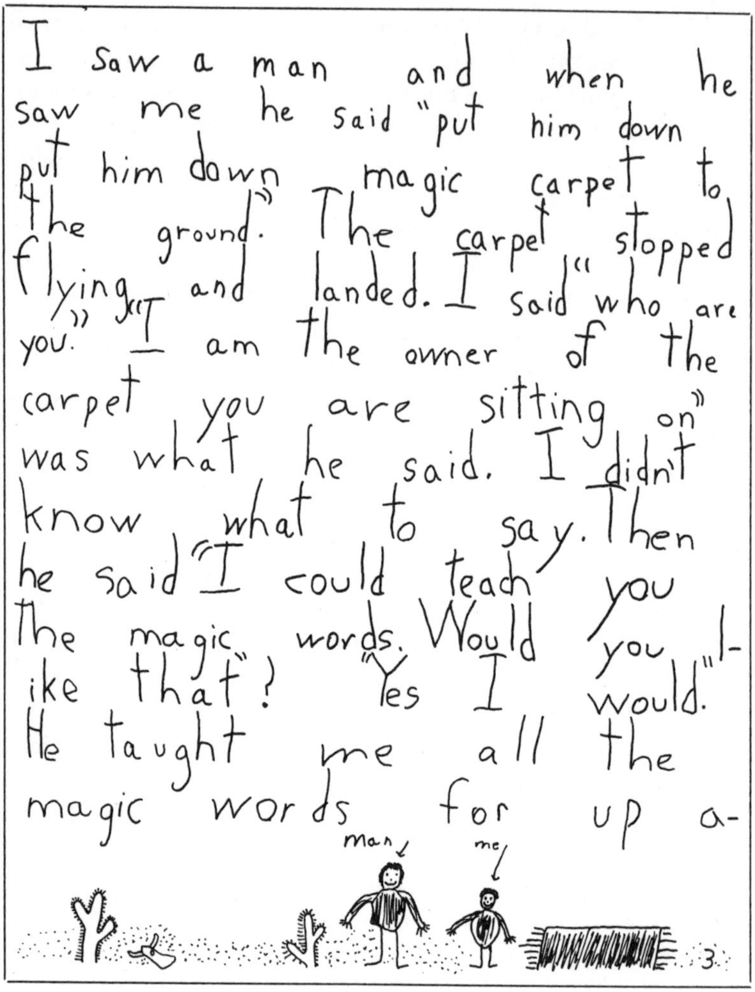

Figure 6.   *Page from "A Magic Carpet or Two" (8:4).*

Once I was playing with two of my best friends Kenny and
Matthew. We were in the attic of Kenny's gararge sorting out
old junk and stuff. Then Kenny's sister Robin came in the
gararge and was going to come up the stairs but we didn't want
her to. We had a system to keep people from coming up. There
was a hole directly above about 1 foot from the first step. There
was a lot of cloth in the attic of the gararge Some pieces big
some small We used the big pieces to keep people from coming
up. We dropped the cloth down the hole. It was going to hit

Robin but then it started flying I grabbed it I got up on it and sat indian style. Then it flew down the steps and out of the gararge. And then it started going what seemed like 100 miles per hour. And before I knew it I was in some strange desert. Then I saw a man and when he saw me he said "put him down put him down magic carpet to the ground." The carpet stopped flying and landed. I said "who are you." "I am the owner of the carpet you are sitting on" was what he said. I didn't know what to say. Then he said "I could teach you the magic words. Would you like that"? "Yes I would." He taught me all the magic words for up and down then I got on waved goodbye and said. "Carpet rise carpet rise fly way up into the skies." and the carpet started flying. I suppose you want to know how you steer a magic carpet well if you want to go right you lift up the front left corner and the opposite for going left. It was almost supper time so I flew home hid my magic carpet in the storage and then I went in to eat my supper.

Chapter II

The next morning was a school day but when I got there we could not go in the classroom because they were putting in a new rug. Finnaly when they were finished the men left. And after a while every body knew that the carpet was wrinkly so Mrs. Mosher called the men and told them what happend. When the men got back they said they needed help then they said. "Who is good at pulling up carpets?" Nobody said anything. And nobody raised their hand exept me so then they said. "Everybody out of the room exept this little boy." Everybody left exept me and the men. Then I said. "Carpet rise carpet rise fly way up into the skies" And the carpet pulled out all the nails and started flying around by itself. Then Mrs. Mosher said. "Line up for lunch." But the carpet went downstairs went through the second grade lunch line and the lunch people put lunches on the carpet and then it flew back to our classroom. "Wow"! everybody yelled out. "It's terrific." Then I said. "Put lunch down put lunch down magic carpet to the ground." And the carpet landed. When everybody had eaten their lunch Mrs. Mosher said "line up for recess." We lined up then we went out to recess. and then spelling and then math and then HOME!

Chapter III

The next morning when I got to school Amanda, Betty, David,

Darren, Lloyd, Louise and Randy were all on the carpet in the air. Then Mrs. Mosher said "Attendance." Everybody got down off the carpet. When Mrs. Mosher finished we had penmanship for a long time. Mrs. Mosher called the men because yesterday the carpet was not nailed down. Then a person said "carpet rise carpet rise fly way up into the skies." And the carpet started flying around the room. Magic carpets sort of have a brain all their own and some how the carpets brains was too exited to listen and started tearing around the room then there was a fire drill the class went out the fire door then the carpet hit the beam in the center of the room and then the beam broke and the whole room collapsed. Then the carpet wrecked the rest of the school building then everybody yelled out "OH NO"!

Third grade introduced Paul to informational writing, first through factual "research" reports; then later in the year he and a friend chose to work with prisms during a time of varied class activities and were each given a notebook to write their findings in. They decided to continue recording information in their books, and Paul added a section on the planets when he brought his home after the school year closed. This was his treasured "Know-It All" book, and after it got lost on the school bus early in his fourth grade year, he grieved it for months. (Fortunately, I had already copied its contents.) It reveals a love of collecting information, strong at this age and reflected in Paul's reading as well, and contains an observational narrative in the first entries that is as unique in Paul's writing as the conditions that produced it: Paul and his friend were given both the equipment and the freedom to make scientific discoveries, the expectation that these discoveries would be recorded, and an enthusiastic response from their teacher. She conveyed no expectation of what discoveries they should make, so they had to find their own questions. Imagine third graders being *asked* to prove with a prism that the earth moves!

> Paul's Know-It All Vol. I (8:7)
>
> p. 1   Mar. 9, 1977
>
> A prism is a thick (mostly) peice of glass that puts the colors of sunlight visible to the human eye.
>
> The average colors a prism reveals are: red, yellow, bluish green, and, purple.
>
> Steve and I proved that the world moves. (See pg. 2.)

The prism is 14 ½ cm. long 4 cm. high on the top it is 1 mm across. and on the bottom it is 4 cm. across.

p. 2   Mar. 9
Steve and I proved that the earth moves.
How we proved it.:
Discovery No. 1 We put the prism on the desk in the sunlight and it projected a rectangle spectrum on the ceiling.
While we were talking and recording the colors of the spectrum (See page 1) We noticed a change in the spectrum. It wasn't a rectangle any more! It was smaller than last time we looked. It was a very thin rectangle!
We couldn't figure out why it had changed shape. We moved everything we could out of the way . . . nothing happened. Then I said "The sun moved!" But then I remembered the sun *couldn't* move and Mrs. Mosher said "No" "The sun *can't* move," so we knew that the earth had moved.

p. 3   Our Discoveries (cont.)
I Discovered that light bounces off the top of a prism and doesn't go through it.
Discovery No. 2
[Discovery number 2 was never described.]

For a child whose language has been so shaped by that of books and educated adults around him that he can independently write "A prism is a thick (mostly) peice of glass that puts the colors of sunlight visible to the human eye," putting a textbook statement or an encyclopedia article into his own words is not difficult. The two "languages" are not that different. But for students who are less surrounded by educated speech and book language, the translation task is of a different order. One such student, explaining to me why he copied directly from the encyclopedia rather than paraphrasing, said "it didn't sound good" (that is, like book language) in his own words.

Like Paul's other books, his "Know-It All" had an index:

5 Insect Study
6 St. Johnsbury Museum
7 Countries
8 Diving water Beetle
9 The Planets

Not only the index itself but the wording of his titles, the use of abbreviations and of such expressions as "(continued)" and "(see page 1)" bespeak his familiarity with informational books.

Both Paul's perspective and his language are objectivized. In the following entry, combining information from several sources, he explains impersonally what he would weigh on the moon: "a child wieghing 65 lbs. would weigh about 12 lbs on the Moon." Decentering is a part of growing up, as Piaget has demonstrated in a number of areas. "Developmentally transactional [informative] writing must depend in some measure on the child's capacity to subordinate himself to the matter in hand" (Burgess et al., 1973, p. 26).

> p. 4   Mass, Gravity, and Wieght (8:10)
> The greater mass of something the more gravity it has.
> The Earth is much bigger than the moon so a person wieghing 180 lbs. on earth would wiegh 30 lbs. on the moon.
> And a child wieghing 65 lbs. would weigh about 12 lbs on the Moon.
> If you could stand on the Sun you could not lift your foot and you would probably be pulled flat down.

Two entries from about this same date reflect science reading Paul had done at school. They are less interesting to read than much of his earlier writing because they are more impersonal and conventional—qualities important for school as well as scientific success. Paul himself indicated the loss of the date.

> p. 5   (Date Lost)
> Insect Studies
> Body shape: Bannana
> color: ligt green
> size: 6mm. lg.   1½mm. wd.
> legs? 6
> antenna? no
> wings? yes
> nose? yes   small, black

eyes? yes   black
mouth? yes
tongue? ??
head? yes
whiskers? no
tail? no
male or female? ??
special features: small orange spots on wings

p. 8 Diving Water beetle
1 ½ in. lg. Enemy of small water creatures, even attacks larger
fish. prey is eaten live. some of air supply in air bubbles beneath
wings. Back legs fringed to work as flippers. Prey is held with
front legs. orange triangle between eyes. bamboo-like antennae. 2 pair of antennae. bottom pair under mouth are shorter.
lives in all parts of world.

Paul was much more selective in deciding on the information
for this entry, based on exhibits about other countries by
students in a fourth grade class. He was amazed by and continued to mention months later the length of China's Great
Wall, the use of caves for apartments in Spain, and the "special
hut" which provided an escape from danger in the bullfights.

p. 7   June 10, 1977 (8:11)
China: rubber tress
great wall: 1500 mil.
Spain: caves for apartments. in bullfight you can go in special
hut.

The little quiz, based on a museum visit, that he included in his
"Know-It All." book was the first of its kind:

p. 6
Q. 1. How much I wiegh on moon.
Q. 2. When St. J. Library was founded and name.
A. 1. 12 lbs.
A. 2. St. J. Anetheum, 1871

As a nine-year-old Paul produced volumes of quizzes on the
movie *Star Wars* (which he was an expert on without having
seen it).

The final entry was written at home just before Paul started
fourth grade. The information came from an educational game

we had (*Space Hop*) which included cards with facts about the planets. It starts:

> p. 9   The Planets (9:1)
> There are *9* planets Orbiting the Sun, Mercury, Venus, Earth, Mars, Jupiter, Saturn, Uranus, Neptune, and Pluto. Each planet farther than one before.

The rest reads like an exercise in sentence combining. *Space Hop* includes these cards about Jupiter:

> Go to the largest planet.
> Go to the planet which has a giant red spot.
> Go to the planet which emits natural radio signals.
> Go to the planet which has twelve moons.

Paul wrote:

> Jupiter, the largest planet, has a giant red spot 6 times the size of the U.S., Jupiter also emits natural radio signals, and has twelve moons.

Beyond just combining statements about a single planet, he observed and stated a surprising contrast between two planets. Although this might be called "sentence combining," it is more fundamentally "relationship discovering." He is working from the inside out (ideas to syntax) rather than from the outside in. The information on the game cards was:

> Go to the smallest planet. (Mercury)
> Go to the planet which is closest to the sun. (Mercury)
> Go to the planet which has the hottest surface. (Venus)

Paul wrote:

> The smallest and closest to the sun is mercury. . . . yet venus has the hottest surface.

This sort of informational writing is closely allied with reading comprehension and reasoning processes.

In his home writings as an eight-year-old, Paul continued all the forms he had written in the year before except for "playing school" things (worksheets, report cards). He invented more names (8:3), this time for chemicals (like "sodium incodate" after he got a chemistry set) and for foods (like "pretscuit" on the menu of ALOKO'S RESTURAUNT, which he operated). His DAILY BLAB newspaper (8:4) contained, in addition to the perennial comics, some new features like puzzles and a "Dear Paul" column. He started enthusiastically on a story, "The Dog who went to the Moon" (8:7), which stylistically resembled "A Magic Carpet or Two." He still wrote signs, directions, notes, lists, rhymes, and plans.

The new form his spontaneous writing took was a diary (started 8:3) which, along with stories, was his main form of expressive writing and his first sustained writing clearly directed to himself alone. He was becoming more and more his own person with his own internal and external worlds. In part through writing, he was assuming responsibility for those worlds; for example, through his diary he was dealing with his feelings, and through his "organizers" with his possessions and actions. DO.NAT KM.IN.ANE.MOR.JST.LETL.KES (Do not come in any more. Just little kids. 5:6) was an early intimation of this maturing.

Paul's third grade school writings, as a whole, stand out more strongly than his home writings that year as indicators of his development. They also provided a fresh stimulus for some spontaneous writing, which hardly occurred during any other year. In fourth grade Paul did a lot of workbook writing, wrote sentences incorporating the week's spelling words, and wrote a few stories (one-day assignments, shorter than his third grade tales and usually turning upon a joke rather than his previous, more organic plot structure), a long Christmas poem, and informational notes from reading about foreign countries. He continued to write at home in a wider range of forms than at school — nearly the same forms he had used the year before.

The following article from his newspaper "The Daily Round-up" (9:0) shows a sense of humor and new, sophisticated elements of style (simile and alliteration). It was typed in newspaper column style:

PISTOL PAUL GONE GUNWACKY
Pistol Paul just
baught a new pi-
stol and is us-

ing up ammo like
a lawn mower
uses up gasoline
   Scientists
say that he must
have a terrible
earwax problem
because anyone
else in his
position would
be deaf by now.
(photo labeled
"Pistol Paul"
affixed here)

The schedule he wrote for himself one afternoon (9:1) again shows his humor as well as greater precision than earlier schedules:

2:00 Go swimming
2:15 Snack
2:30 Mow lawn
2:50 Snack
3:00 Archery
3:30 Snack
3:35 Work on model
4:00 Watch TV
4:30 Snack
4:35 Write letters
4:50 MONEY hunt and totaling Money
5:15 Snack
5:16 Get crabbed at by Mother [for eating before supper implied?]
5:18 Do whatever I want until supper

And this one, some seven months later (9:8), more fully grafts expressive writing to a routine transactional form:

SCHEDULE FOR TODAY

Easter Sunday

Do all of Italy facts
Clean room
Do STAR WARS stuff

Clean room more until finished
Do STAR WARS stuff until supper
Eat supper
Eat dessert
Get full
Lie on couch if daddy isn't there
Finish getting full
Try to get on couch again
Do STAR WARS stuff and lissen to dat radiola!
Brush toofies
Get in bed
Go beddy bye!
ZZZZZZZZZZZZZZZZZZZZZZ...............

I had asked Paul to make out a schedule in hopes I could avoid nagging him to get necessary (in my view) work done; namely, cleaning his room and finishing his assignment on Italy. The proportion of space devoted to this work on his schedule suggests a difference in our points of view. The "schedule," in fact, was yet another way of declining the work.

To suggest the range of possibilities within the schedule form, compare Paul's light-hearted lists with this serious, at times sharply detailed narrative plan written by his eight-year-old friend Matthew for a day they were going to spend together:

GO TO MY OWLD HOUIS AND WORK ON OWR FORTS EAT A LITTIL AND WOLK TO THE BRIGE AND THEROH ROKE'S IN AND GO TO PAULE'S AGEN AND GO TO THE SHOGER HOUIS AND PRITEN A-ROBER WAS FOELOING US WITH HONTING DOG'S AND THEN GO BAKE UP TO HAVE LONCH AND THEN DO WOUT EVER WE WONT
(Go to my old house and work on our forts eat a little and walk to the bridge and throw rocks in and go to Paul's again and go to the sugar house and pretend a robber was following us with hunting dogs and then go back up to have lunch and then do whatever we want.)

Matthew, an artistic child, concluded his plan with an expressive drawing of two smiling boys, each with an arm around the other's shoulder.

Paul's business enterprise as a nine-year-old was "Paul's Flea

Market," for which he wrote signs, advertisements, and catalogues. His close imitation of commercial advertising is evident in his announcement (9:4) reproduced in figure 7.

Above this time he also wrote "A Very Small Book of Calculator Games," giving instructions for games he devised. He did not seem troubled that no one played the games, but was satisfied with his *product*, especially his illustrations of calculators. He had a resurgence of letter writing—to friends, which were notably longer than letters he had written when younger, and business letters for mail order items like magic tricks and free information. Addressing his writing to such an unknown, impersonal audience was new for Paul. As the following example (9:5) shows, he had been instructed in basic letter form but not yet in all the depersonalized wording of a business request. He asked me about the salutation, suggesting himself that it might be "Dear Sir" or "Sirs."

Jan. 7, 1977

Dear Sirs,
Your metric information sounds like a very handy thing to have. So please send me one.
    My adress is: (address label affixed here)
        Your customer,
        Paul Bissex

The new influence on Paul's writing as a nine-year-old came from his peer group and culture—another benchmark of his growing up. When quiz contests were the rage among his schoolmates, he also wrote some at home. He wrote codes and membership cards for his clubs. And the *Star Wars* film— although he had not seen it when it first came around—led to massive reading, writing, and collecting efforts (starting 9:7), which he shared with his equally *Star Wars*-struck friends. He typed out long sections from the novel (one of the rare times he copied print verbatim), compiled information from magazine articles and *Star Wars* cards, and produced many tiny booklets of "Star Wars Quizzes." His first one (excerpted below) covered all aspects of the movie; later booklets each focused on an individual character.

ANNOUNCING

Paul's Flea Market is having a

Clearance Sale to make

Room for new products!

SAVE!

Prices Slashed!

Savings up to 4¢!

COME NOW!

Figure 7. *"Announcement" (9:4).*

THE STAR WARS MINI QUIZ BOOK By Paul Bissex
   0. Who is the writer?
   1. Who is the director?
   2. Who is the producer?
   3. Who is Darth Vader?
   4. About how many different kinds of explosions were there?
   5. Who made Darth Vader's voice?
   6. What is R2-D2?

7. What is C3-PO?
8. What is Han Solo's ship called?
9. Why does Darth Vader wear a mask?
10. Who wrote the music?
(and so on)

Although he quizzed his parents and friends with some of these, and said he wrote them with such an intent, they were also *objets d'art*—each booklet decorated with his minute and detailed drawings plus cutouts from *Star Wars* cards, stored in a small box that was decorated inside and out, and placed on his *Star Wars* shelf, itself highly decorated and organized. As a "research project," this eclipsed any he did at school.

The samples of eight- and nine-year-old writing presented in this section show Paul well on his way to mastering English spelling, including some of its finer discriminations. Much of his spelling development can be seen through a list Paul made of "HARD WORDS (to spell)" (8:7) and through the evolution of his *-tion* spelling, which he mastered as an eight-year-old.

Paul had the correct spellings of several *-tion* words in his first grade dictionary, and he had written POLLUTION, SUCTION, and INVENTION in school stories. Although this English spelling is predictable, it was apparently too far from the alphabetic principle on which Paul had been operating— that is, it was too indirectly related to sound—for him to assimilate it as a six-year-old. The sound of "sh" was represented by SH in his mind (which is probably why he still had trouble as an eight-year-old with "ma*ch*ine"). The relation between the spelling *-tion* and the sound "shun" was so remote to Paul that in his reading as late as 7:7 (when he was writing -TOIN) he did not correctly sound out unfamiliar words ending in *-tion*—although he had easily recognized familiar *-tion* words since before he was six years old. The evolution of his spellings for "directions" tells the story:

DRAKTHENS (5:7)
DRAKSHINS (5:8)
DIRECKSHONS (7:5)
DIREKSHONS (7:5)
DIRECTIONS but not sure if the ending was OI or IO (8:1)
DIRECTIONS without question (8:7)

For almost a year (7:5-8:4), Paul used the OI spelling and then, uncertainly, IO: COLECTOIN and IDENTAFACAI-TOIN (7:5); EXAMANATOIN, EDUICATOIN, and MUCITOIN (musician, 7:9); DIRECTIONS (but not sure it was correct, 8:1). Paul was aware of his difficulty and mentioned to me (8:4) that he still had trouble spelling these words because he spelled them -OIN. As suggested before, this seems to have been an interference effect from his early established OI spellings: NOIS (6:5), TOILET (7:6). Paul claimed he had mastered *-tion* because of my corrections and thought his third grade teacher had corrected him too. This pattern was not treated in his third grade spelling book. Apropos of an exercise in his reading workbook on words ending in *-tain, -sion,* and *-tion,* Paul commented to me (8:7) that "confu*sion* and elec*tion* don't sound exactly alike," so his spellings of OCCATIONAL-LY and EXPLOTION (also 8:7) were not due to inability to distinguish the sound of "zhun" from "shun") but rather to overgeneralizing his hard-won knowledge. (He did make the *-tion/-sion* distinction in his nine-year-old spellings.) No wonder so many *-tion* words appeared on Paul's HARD WORDS list (8:7):

HARD WORDS (to spell)

antidisestablishmenterianism		
satisfaction	complicated	
carbonated	scientific	
corrosive	character	
exploition	exploraition	
developed	interesting	extinct
antimated	fictional	puncuation
individual	annahilliated	
irrataitional	antimated	intellectual

ANTIDIS*A*STABLISHMENT*A*RIANISUM had been his first attempt at this word three months earlier. He said he used *A,* in the italicized places, because "uh" is often written *A.* When he asked if it was correct, I explained his two errors, which he changed; but ever after he has put *E*'s where *both* of the original *A*'s were. His spellings of unstressed vowels in this word list (as in sat*i*sfaction, compl*i*cated, carb*o*nated) are all correct but one (irr*a*taitional). Since they cannot be sounded out—and since in most cases related forms of the words which stress these vowels do not exist—Paul must be depending on visual recall.

His "hard words" show a knowledge of prefixes and suffixes:

Prefixes	Suffixes	
anti	ment	al
dis	ian	ual
com (cor)	ism	ed
ex	tion	ing
de	ate	
in	(if)ic	

His writings during the year evidenced knowledge of other suffixes: *-cide, -ible, -ity, -ure, -age,* and *-ine.*

Paul is accurate about doubled consonants: CO*RR*OSIVE, I*RR*ATAITIONAL, INTE*LL*ECTUAL. The only instruction he had had up to this time about doubling was to double final consonants before a suffix starting with a vowel. AN-NAHILLIATED derives from a humorous mispronunciation on a recording of an old Fibber McGee radio show; I do not know if he ever saw "annihilated" in print. The omitted *t* in PUNCUATION probably derives from Paul's pronunciation; he uses the *nct* cluster correctly in EXTINCT (which he so pronounces). ANTIMATED he had a month or so earlier tried out two ways on paper: ANIMATED, then ANTI-MATED—which he perhaps judged to be correct by faulty analogy with the prefix "anti."

Paul knows the silent consonants in S*C*IENTIFIC and C*H*ARACTER. His awareness of silent consonants is not new; at 7:9, when he heard the word "fillet," he asked, "Doesn't 'fillet' have a silent letter at the end of it? A consonant? I forget what it is." Now he was better able to remember what those silent consonants were. Sometimes he was still unable to believe them, as when he erased the *T* from LISTEND in a story he had written (8:3). However, his spelling progress beyond the alphabetic principle is clear from his grasp of affixes, doubled and silent consonants, and more accurate representations of unstressed vowels. His eight-year-old spellings usually take position in word and letter environment into account in representing sounds (for example, the "ng" sound in EX-

TINCT is conventionally spelled without a *g*, and the "sh" sound in PUNCUATION is spelled *TI*).

I assume Paul intended IRRATAITIONAL as a form of "irritate." Both this spelling and EXPLORAITION indicate he does not know that *any* vowel (not just *e*) can give the long sound to a preceding stressed vowel followed by a single consonant, though he did in PUNCU*A*TION.

Paul's first spelling of "explosion" was EXPLOTION, but he said it didn't look right so he tried adding the *I*: EXPLOITION. His usual correction strategy is to identify misspellings visually (they don't look right) and then try out alternative spellings. Sometimes his repertoire of alternatives does not include the requisite one. The questions he asked about spelling—which were few this year—usually posed alternatives: One or two *s*'s in "desert"? Is "motorcycle" with an *i* or a *y*? Is "machine" m-a-s-c-i-n-e or m-a-c-i-n-e? Are there two *t*'s in "nighttime"?

This "hard word" list does not demonstrate Paul's mastery of the *au* and *ie* combinations, which were not established in his spellings as a seven-year-old.

I gave him some spelling words to see whether he could recover unstressed vowels and silent consonants through other forms of the word in which they were pronounced. At 8:9 he spelled these words and gave these explanations for his spellings:

Words given	Paul's spelling if nonstandard	Paul's comments
conserve		Just spelled it like it sounds.
inspiration		Did think of "inspire."
injury		Just knew it.
industry		Just knew it.
ridiculous		I saw it in my *You Are Ridiculous* book (which he had read when much younger).
courageous	courageos	I was just thinking of "courage." Also thought *e* was needed to make the long *a*.
temperature		When I see a (unpredictable) word and want to spell it, I say it in a kind of funny way, like pee-oh-plee (people) and temper-ay-ture.
majority		Knew *a* because of "major." I don't know

		what the word means but I've heard it in "majority rule."
criticism	criticizm	*c* because of criti*c*; *z* because of critici*z*e.
muscle		I've seen it before.
sign		I've read it many times.
medicine		He said afterwards *c* as in "medical" but was not conscious of this while spelling.

Much of Paul's spelling ability cannot be accounted for in terms of what he has been systematically taught. He learned from corrections and from his own questions. Above all, probably, he learned from his considerable reading — not automatically because the words were before his eyes, but because as a writer he was attentive to and interested in spellings.

So many of Paul's nine-year-old spellings were correct that evidence of his further knowledge of spelling could not be fully observed by reading over his writings. From them it was clear that he was continuing to extend his spelling knowledge in the ways he had as an eight-year-old. He was aware of more uncommon alternative patterns and took more account of environmental constraints. To try to uncover more of his knowledge and limits, I gave him another list of spelling words (9:8):

Words given	Paul's spelling if nonstandard	Paul's comments
suspicious		
contagious	contagous	Said he had not seen this word, as he had seen "suspicious," which he spelled correctly. (Not aware of vowels that affect the pronunciation of *g* — less predictably than *c*, which he handled correctly in all other words: so*c*ialism, spheri*c*al, authenti*c*; cf. SPESHEL (7:3).
authentic		
socialism		
finally		
ointment		
spherical		"I don't even know the word — how'm I supposed to spell it?" (He was outraged but did, however, think of "sphere.") "It's harder to tell if a word looks right if you don't know the word."
knead		
stomachache		

listened
druggist
exciting   exiting   (He still has not "seen" the *c* in this word that he surely comes across often in reading.)

Three months earlier (9:5), Paul had spelled "exciting" and "except" and listed possible alternative spellings to the italicized ones, which he considered correct: *EXITING,* EXITEING, EKSITING; *EXCEPT,* EXSEPT, EKSEPT, ECSEPT, EC-CEPT. Clearly he is able to think of alternative spellings, both phonetically based (EKSEPT) and by analogy (ECCEPT: accept). Without an available repertoire of alternatives, correction of errors would be impossible.

Paul's spellings of the list of words I gave him at 9:8 indicate:

Spelling knowledge of these affixes: *-ous, -ic, -ism, -al, -ly, -ment, -ist, sus-, con-.*

Ability to distinguish homonyms (knead), which he has been very alert to and interested in for two or three years already. He has understood that the same spoken word can be represented differently because of a difference in meaning, and he has also been aware of multiple meanings without spelling changes since about age seven.

Consonant doubling: druggist, finally.

Functional knowledge of the effect of vowel environment on the pronunciation of *c*: socialism, suspicious, spherical, authentic.

Awareness of uncommon spelling patterns: stomachache.

Observance of environmental constraints: *ph* (not *f*) for "f" after *s* in "spherical."

Paul's own "List of Long Words" (9:8), which my spelling list inspired, further shows his near mastery of many Latinate morphemes:

antidisestablishmenterianism	regularity
discombobulated	orginization
permanently	reincarnation
simularities	humiliate
combustable	collectable
dematerialize	collapsable
commercialization	informative
intergalactic	irregular
electricity	international

What Paul has learned about spelling as a nine-year-old does
not seem to differ *in kind* from what he learned when eight. For
example, he has learned more subtleties of silent letters (col-
um*n*s, spag*h*etti, s*w*ord). He has made some finer discriminations (calculat*o*r and direct*o*r but produc*e*r, and so forth). He
continues to become aware of more uncommon spelling alternatives and of more environmental constraints on spelling. He
has asked very few questions about how to spell words this
year. His spelling work at school has been based on word lists.
He is deducing principles for himself or learning them from
conversations with me. He knows the system and its basic
rules; what he has left to learn are further refinements and
discriminations as well as historical and etymological reasons
for spellings.

Paul's mastery of spelling is expressed in the confidence and
keenness with which he detects spelling errors in printed
material. His mastery is also expressed in orthographic playfulness as in this little piece (9:5):

STAR TREK
  has
phasers
  and
photon torpedos
phor
phoiling
  bad guys

and more sustained foolery (also 9:5):

Joyn thuh Phun with thuh Phamlee Phun knite

Bawgul (Boggle)	with: Gayms
Anagramz	20 kweschens
Munopulee	pompom mayking
Tidelee Wingks	singing
Spas hop	myusik
Pik up stiks	reeding
Net Rezults	oragamee
uther things twoo!	Phunnee Phases (Faces)
Thats tooknite!	speling lesunz
	and much much mowr

Many of these misspellings parody the oversimplified alphabetic approach of Paul's early spelling days, with sounds patterned to letters without regard for environments (for example, JOYN with the diphthong "oi" as it is spelled only at the end of syllables) and without regard for meaningful units (for example, the morphemes *quest* and *-ion* in KWESCHENS or the plural marker *-s* in LESUNZ). Other misspellings are based on his knowledge of less common spelling patterns, as in PHAMLEE PHUN KNITE. He also pokes fun at the spelling of unstressed vowels in such words as MUNOPULEE.

This has been a long journey through five years of a child's writings and all the growing in thought and knowledge, in interests and activities, in relations with the world and with himself that is inseparable from those writings. After all that distance, the beginnings may have dimmed and details may stand out more clearly than the basic shape of the route taken. To try to make that shape clearer, the next chapter will review the evolution of Paul's writing through summary comments and selected examples of both spellings and written forms.

5 Summary

Paul as a Speller

The Beginning of Invented Spelling (5:1-5:3)

Paul took spelling to be systematic and alphabetic. His first job as a speller was to represent speech sounds rather than whole words. In his system, all letters were relational (that is, had their own sounds); there were no markers. Vowel letters necessarily represented more than one sound, but alternative pronunciations were not determined by letter environment. His categories for vowel sounds, as reflected in his spellings, were sometimes different from adult categories.

EFUKANOPNKAZIWILGEVUAKANOPENR   (5:2)
(If you can open cans I will give you a can opener.)

Independent Invented Spelling (5:3-5:9)

During this period Paul mastered and refined his alphabetic system. He was also moving beyond it as shown by his awareness of morphemes (*-s, -ing*), of alternative spellings (c-a-t, k-a-t), of markers ("silent *e*") and of "correct" spelling. "The development from phonetic to morphophonemic is not a direct move

96

from phonetic to adult spelling; rather, there is a dramatic change in the type of (non-adult) spelling the child creates" (Read, 1971, p. 27).

RE.PORT KARD. ON. SPORTS. NAME. PAUL.
PAUL. IS. GOWING. TO. RUN. A. RAWND. AND.
JUMP. AND. EXRSIZ. (5:8)

Toward Conventional Spelling (5:10-6:11, First Grade)

Paul's shift to a visual strategy from a sound-transcribing approach meant he was now focusing on whole words and was equipped to deal with phonetically unpredictable spellings. His spellings of short vowel sounds became conventionalized and, abandoning letter-name strategy, he increased his repertoire of conventional alternatives for representing long vowel sounds. He showed some awareness of environmental constraints, as he could now that he was not just spelling left to right, phoneme by phoneme; for the sound correspondences of letters are usually affected by following rather than preceding letters. He used doubled consonants without understanding the principle, and an increased number of conventionally spelled affixes (*-ed, -er, un-*).

INGREDEINS
2 CUP'S OF FLOUR
1 CUP OF HONY
1 EGG
1 SCUP OF BUTER
WHAT TO DO.
BEET UP WITH BETER (6:8)

Toward Conventional Spelling (7:0-7:11, Second Grade)

Next, Paul enlarged his repertoire of alternative spelling patterns and morphemes. He mastered some common vowel combinations, struggled with silent consonants, and more or less eliminated unacceptable letter sequences from his spellings.

I WILL TYPE SOME WORDS   (7:6)
TYRANNASAURYS REX   LAHGFING
GARBAGE   HILAROUS   NOGGIN
TELEFONE   INDAN   TYPERITER

Basic Mastery of Conventional Spelling (8:0-8:11, Third Grade)

During this year Paul mastered common vowel combinations and consonant doubling. He had a spelling knowledge of
many affixes, including *-tion*. His awareness of environmental
constraints increased, and he showed further mastery of silent
consonants and less common spelling patterns (such as *ph*).
Unstressed vowels were often spelled correctly through visual
recall or recovery of stressed forms. If spellings did not look
right, Paul experimented with alternatives; and he developed a
mispronunciation strategy to remember spelling demons.

> From "The Dog Who Went to the Moon"   (8:7)
> ½ hour later: Sugar and her master entered a large room filled
> with people and their pets, dogs, cats, genaua pigs, and even
> goldfish! Then a man walked right into the room and said:
> "May I have your attention please?" Everybody stopped talking
> at once. Why? It was the president! "I have called this meeting
> so we can choose which animal to give the privelage of being the
> first creature to the moon and back." Now of course as soon as
> the goldfish owners heard this they left. (You can probably
> guess the reason.)

Refining Conventional Spelling (9:0-9:11, fourth grade)

Through the same processes by which he had basically mastered conventional spelling, Paul continued to extend his
knowledge, particularly of less common spelling patterns and
of the spellings of polysyllabic Latin and even Greek derivatives, which were an increasing part of his vocabulary.

> A List of Long Words   (9:8)
>
> | | |
> |---|---|
> | antidisestablishmenterianism | regularity |
> | discombobulated | orginization |
> | permanently | reincarnation |
> | simularities | humiliate |
> | combustable | collectable |
> | dematerialize | collapsable |
> | commercialization | informative |
> | intergalactic | irregular |
> | electricity | international |

These spellings show how far Paul has progressed from his invented spelling strategy—from phonemic transcription of

speech sounds using surface sound-letter correspondences —
toward representing words using a morphophonemic system in
which sound-letter relationships are mediated by meaning. In
his list of words he appropriately represented the "sh" sound by
sh (antidisestabli*sh*menterianism), *ci* (commer*ci*alization), and
ti (as in orginiza*ti*on). He also correctly represented the long *e*
sound by *y* (as in permanentl*y*), *ie* (simulariti*e*s), *i* (as in
humil*i*ate), and *e* (as in d*e*materialize).

As an inventive speller, Paul operated on a belief that spelling was systematic; he learned the basic sound-letter correspondences and came to use conventional spellings for a few
common morphemes. Although his spellings, before he entered
first grade, were in some ways still far from conventional, the
foundation of his later spelling development was established.
(Some much older children with severe spelling problems are
no further along than this in their understanding of English orthography.) Paul's shift to visual strategies as a six-year-old
facilitated his development as a speller during the years following. He came to learn more and more variant spelling patterns
and to take into account more conditions determining the
choice among patterns. He acquired a store of sight morphemes, including an increasing array of Latinate and Greek
ones. His attention to word meanings (which will be more evident when his vocabulary growth is described in Chapter 10)
furthered his spelling development through his awareness of
morphemes and homonyms.

Though Paul received formal spelling instruction at school
and informal instruction at home, this was not enough to explain his full development as a speller. In this Paul is not
remarkable, but typical: most children's functional spelling
knowledge could not be accounted for merely on the basis of
the workbook exercises and spelling lists they have performed.
Paul's history serves to make more obvious Read's contention
that "what the child learns in mastering the spelling system is a
representation related in complex, but generally systematic,
ways to the phonology of English. The contrary assumption — that the child memorizes a long list of generally unpredictable spellings — fails to account for the abilities of mature
readers and writers" (Read, 1971, p. 3).

In another view, inventive spellers start from the assumption that they can figure things out for themselves. Perhaps this is why so many of them learn to read before formal instruction. In her study of characteristics contributing to the development of scientists, Anne Roe remarked on the importance of their youthful discovery that they could find things out for themselves. She also noted that this discovery "is not a natural part of growing up for every child in our culture" (Roe, 1952, p. 238). This issue will be explored further in Chapter 6.

Paul as a Writer: Forms, Functions, and Themes

The kinds of writing Paul has done over the years of this study are shown in the table below. The categories are descriptive rather than systematic. The category of "little books" overlaps with some others, but I have left it in because the book format has had such a strong appeal for Paul throughout these years, with some books created more as written or decorative "objects" than as texts. This reflects the closeness of writing and

Forms of writing	Ages				
PERSISTENT FORMS	5	6	7	8	9
signs, labels, captions	X	X	X	X	X
stories	X	X	X	X	X
little books	X	X	X	X	X
directions	X	X	X	X	X
lists or catalogues	X	X	X	X	X
newspapers	(X)	X	X	X	X
notes, letters, greeting cards	X	X	X	X	X
DISCONTINUED FORMS					
"statements"	X				
school-type exercises	X	X	X		
riddles		X	continued		
			orally		
LATER FORMS					
rhymes		X	X	X	X
charts, organizers and planners			X	X	X
diary				X	X
quizzes (information in Q & A form)				X	X
informational and observational notebook				X	X
codes					X

drawing, both for children and in the history of writing. Illustrations, illuminated letters, and expressive graphics like deliberate variations in letter size and line and spacing have almost invariably been a part of Paul's writing.

For whom did Paul write? And for what purposes? Conventional categories may not apply to the writings of young children, who do not see the world as adults do and do not make the same distinctions. Understanding the purposes of a child's writing means understanding his view of himself and the world.

Paul's early writings seemed to involve at once the accomplishment of writing something at all—the competence and power of the act of writing—interest in the written object, and a desire that the substance of the writing be shared (that I read it or he read it to me). As a five-year-old he was still absorbed in naming, in knowing his world by naming its parts; through his signs and labels and captions he extended this process in writing. In the next year or two, as his reasoning developed and his need to know and control the world around him became expressed through categorizing, this process was reflected in his charts and other organizational writings.

In stories he elaborated themes of persistence, power, and control, often setting himself and his friends in worlds of unusual adventure and challenge. In writing verse he enjoyed the satisfaction of making rhymes and patterns with language. In his accumulations of informational writing (like his "Know-It All" book) he had tangible evidence of his growing knowledge of the world. He wrote letters mostly to get things done. He wrote a diary perhaps to confirm the reality of the emerging world of his private experiences and feelings. He wrote as a spectator and as a participant.

Across the forms of Paul's writings runs a characteristic inventiveness—an experimenting, a playfulness, a delight in construction: elaborating, combining, altering existing forms rather than just imitating them. This inventiveness was evident in the plots of his later stories as well as in his adaptations of such adult forms as newspapers and schedules. It also characterized his play activities during this period.

Development in general appears to proceed from global to

increasingly differentiated functions and awareness. Hand in hand with differentiation goes decentration, that moving beyond egocentricity which Piaget has traced down so many avenues. In Paul's early writing there was no clear distinction between writer and audience. Although some messages were written for me as a person, they were not written to me as an audience unable to share automatically all the writer's unexpressed knowledge. Later, when he wrote "A Magic Carpet or Two," Paul was aware that a reader might have questions about some aspects of the story, and he addressed himself explicitly and implicitly to those questions. He could stand outside his writing—outside his understanding of what he had written.

Paul came to differentiate not only writer and audience, but also various kinds of audiences: peers, teachers, parents, strangers (in business letters), and self (in diaries). As part of his growing up, Paul carried on transactions with a widening audience—from Federal offices in Washington, D.C., to magazine editors in New York, to friends in other states, to his close friends and family. He was polite and businesslike in his business letters, could sound quite bookish in his school writings, was teasing and humorous with his parents and so on. His sense of audience and style as well as his purposes in writing became increasingly differentiated and transformed as Paul grew older.

Two persistent forms in Paul's writing have been newspapers and stories. In viewing the evolution of those particular forms, we can recapitulate some of the main lines of development in his writing and see the transformations more clearly by moving rapidly from year to year.

Newspapers

5:1   First attempt, involving something about Peanuts, scrapped because of a spelling problem.

5:7   TIMS. R.GIS   (Times Argus
        THAR. WL. B. SHAWRS.   There will be showers
        IN. THE. AFTR.NUN   in the afternoon.)
        (Picture of raindrops captioned RAN.)

6:7   FUNE'S (Two single-frame cartoons: one of a person spitting on another who protests "PIG," and the other of several figures shooting at an airplane overhead.)

THE SAFTERNEWN IT'S GOING TO RAIN. (Picture of two people with umbrellas under dripping raincloud.)

IT'S GOING TO BE FAIR TOMORRO (Picture of two people under SHINING SUN.)

BIG SALE! TODAY AT MAKEER'S (illustration)

GET FISH! AT SEA SCOLAPS (illustration)

1 OF THE BASEBALL TEME'S HIT A HOME RUN YESTERDAY.

8:4   THE DAILY BLAB NEWSPAPER 11-17-76

FUN! !COMIX!COMIX!COMIX! Two 2-frame cartoons:

1. BLABBY is standing by an open manhole with a MEN sign beside it, saying "I WISH I COULD SEE UNDERGROUND." In the second frame he has disappeared and his voice rises from the dark manhole: "MY WISH CAME TRUE!"

2. EDDY is greeted by another figure who slaps him (THUMP) saying, "HI ED HOW YA DOIN." ED says "OOF" and in the next frame, lying flat on the ground, says "FINE."

ATTENTION! THE TWINFEILD BOOSTERS CLUB IS HAVING A SKI AND SKATE SALE AT TWINFEILD HIGH-SCHOOL IN THE CAFETERIA ON SATURDAY, NOVEM (copied from a school notice and left unfinished)

AS THE BOY SITS THERE CAN YOU FIND A, SAW, TIC-TAC-TOE BOARD, BALL (objects hidden in design surrounding figure sitting on a chair)

ANYTHING IN PARTICULAR THAT YOU WANT THIS CHRISTMAS?

JUST SEND IT TO: CHRISTMAS PRESENTS 2ND ST. 02234

DEAR, PAUL CAN AWNSER (left unfinished)

9:1   THE DAILY ROUNDUP   AUGUST 2, 1977

PISTOL PAUL GONE GUNWACKY

Pistol Paul just
baught a new pi-
stol and is us-
ing up ammo like
a lawn mower
uses up gasoline
   Scientists
say that he must
have a terrible
earwax problem
because anyone
else in his
position would
be deaf by now.
(Photograph of Pistol Paul beneath article.)
Daily Doings
afternoon:store opens at 4:30 and a magic show at
5:00.
night:Family game of MNOPOLY.
(Newspaper left unfinished.)

The variety of sections in Paul's newspapers expanded from
the newspaper name and an illustrated weather forecast (5:7)
to include advertising, funnies, sports news, notices of a forthcoming event, a puzzle, a request column, Dear Paul, and a
humorous human interest story. At first his "news" was entirely
invented, but his eight- and nine-year-old papers include actual events. THE DAILY ROUNDUP (9:1) is much more
realistic in format as well, with a column heading, narrow column, and photo of the subject of the article. His humor grows
more sophisticated and verbal (compare the Pistol Paul article
with his earlier "funnies"). The parody in "Pistol Paul" recalls
Mad magazine, which Paul has adored since he was seven years
old.

Stories

5:1	WANS	WAN	AD	AWA	RKA
	APNA	SA	THTB	AD E	MBK
	TMTAR	BAR	AR WAT	ENAV	AGAN
	(Once	wa-	and	away	er ca-
	upon a	s a	that b-	and he	me back
	time there	bear	ear went	(he) nev-	again)

One of Paul's very early compositions was this little story with the conventional beginning, in which a single character performs a single action—the barest bones of a story.

The stories he wrote the following year were done in school, beneath drawings he had made, like this one:

6:7　　THIS IS THE POLICE CHASING ME AND I AM GOING TO GO UP A RAMP AND I AM GOING TO LAND IN A HOLE AND THE HOLE IS MY HIDEOUT.

There are now two characters, a conflict, and a sequence of actions—still pretty bare bones. But the next year there are real characters, in a defined setting, with motivations and feelings that account for the more extended and complicated chain of events. A hero with a goal meets an obstacle, which he overcomes:

7:6　　ONCE APON A TIME THERE WAS A LIT-TLE RABIT HOW HAD NO HOME. SO HE LOOKED FOR ONE IN THE DISTANCE HE COULD SEE A LIGHT HE WENT TOWARD IT IT WAS A HOUSE AT LAST HE HAD A HOME!! HE WENT IN THIS IS WHAT IT LOOKED LIKE (drawing of the interior) THEN A MAN CAME OUT OF A DOOR AND TOOK THE RABIT OUT THE RABIT CAME BACK TO THE HOUSE THIS TIME THE MAN FELT SORRY FOR THE RABIT AND LET THE RABIT IN AND THE RABIT AND THE MAN LIVED HAPPLY EVER AFTER　THE END

The rabbit story is a transition between simple, childish narratives and an elaborated piece of youthful literature, "A Magic Carpet or Two" (8:4), quoted earlier on pages 75-78. "A Magic Carpet or Two" presents a cast of (relatively) thousands, moving across four settings (Kenny's garage, the strange desert, school, and home). The smooth transitions between the real and magical worlds create a dreamlike intermingling of the strange with the familiar. Throughout the story, the everyday world (of school, home, play) with its order and predictability is contrasted with the magical world of the carpet, which breaks down boundaries and structures and expectations. The ending, in its ambiguity, is much more complex than the endings of Paul's earlier stories. Instead of straight narration, he uses a combination of dramatization, dialogue, and narrative—more recreating than telling about. We are aware of the storyteller as well as the story—a storyteller with skillful control of his material, a sense of humor, and awareness of his audience. A similar growth of complexity in characters, plot, setting, and tone is evident in literature as we move from young children's books toward adult novels.

Other forms that might be traced for several years through Paul's writings show similar lines of development: toward complexity of structure within pieces of greater length, specificity of detail, and a distinct, conscious, and sometimes multifaceted attitude toward his content.

Paul as an eight-year-old has greater skills as a writer because spelling and handwriting are now quite automatic, he has had much practice in developing a variety of forms, and he has done a lot of reading which contributed to his writing repertoire. But the nature of his development in writing also reflects his greater knowledge of the world, his decentering (expressed both in his absorption of things outside himself and in his ability to consider other points of view), and the growth of his imagination (as distinct from childish "distortions" of "reality") and reasoning. He is able to take a broader, more comprehensive view of life. Longitudinal descriptions and analyses of children's productions are thus at the same time essays in child development.

Parallels between Paul's writing and reading interests, in both forms and content, are described in Part III. More broadly viewed, "writing interests" and "reading interests" are expressions of personal, developmental themes and styles, expressed also through other aspects of a child's life such as his play and social activities. For example, Paul's needs as an eight- and nine-year-old for independence, autonomy, and personal mastery of the environment—qualities that Roe (1952) observed as being prevalent among scientists—are manifest in the themes of "A Magic Carpet or Two" (his mastery of the carpet, the carpet's ultimate independence), in his organizational schedules and charts and plans, through his devouring of factual information in reading (e.g., the *Guinness Book of World Records*), in his love of adventure stories like the *Tintin* series, and his interest in breaking codes and solving mysteries. His need for autonomy and mastery is further expressed in his activities: through performing magic tricks, through his resistance to adult scheduling demands at school and at home (unless he can provide his own motivation for working within them), and through a related process of setting up challenges for himself to do more difficult or rapid physical or mental activities, like timed running or reading.

Paul clearly wanted to learn to write. But the forms and contents and occasions of his writings also mattered to him, the strength of these patterns emerging only over time. At the start, learning to write in itself had meaning for Paul as for his parents and teachers. I wonder how alike or how different those meanings — for instance, of personal accomplishment or cultural participation — may have been. Although Paul was proud that he *could* write, writing never seemed only an end in itself, a self-justifying activity. Paul, like his parents, wrote (and read and talked) because what he was writing (or reading or saying) had meaning to him as an individual and as a cultural being. We humans are meaning-making creatures, and language — spoken and written — is an important means for making and sharing meanings.

6 Educational Implications

Implications for Writing

The development of writing, as seen in this case study, was part of the development of the person rather than the product of an instructional writing skills sequence. Of course, information, models, assignments, and responses were provided by Paul's home and school environment; the writing did not develop spontaneously in a vacuum. In his independent writings, Paul selected what he wanted to use from his environment; for example, he imitated or adapted some—but only *some*—of the written forms he was exposed to.

One basic direction, already mentioned, in the development of Paul's writing was what Piaget has called decentration—moving outward from an egocentric view of the world. By the time Paul wrote his magic carpet story, he was very conscious of audience, of what needed to be explained to someone else. Such a growing awareness of audience in young writers of this age (Paul was eight) has been noted by Graves (1978b). Another form of decentering, also noted by Graves (1975) especially for young boy writers, was a reaching beyond their immediate spheres of home and school to the larger community, current events, and so on for subject matter. For letter writing, Paul's audience expanded from family and friends to unknown clerks (business letters). Reflecting his growth in logical thinking, Paul's writing came to include more impersonal forms—organizational and informational writing. This is the line of development traced by recent British researchers (for example, Martin, 1967): from personal to impersonal uses of language, from narrative to expository writing.

Such a developmental view of writing implies that learning comes from growth as well as instruction, and it outlines kinds of progressions that teachers might expect to observe and foster in the work of young elementary school writers.

The spatial dimension of decentering in terms of audience and subject matter, already mentioned as a major pattern in Paul's writing, was complemented by a temporal dimension as he engaged in more writing projects that he sustained or returned to over weeks and even months (his magic carpet story, "Know-It All" book, diary, *Star Wars* quizzes). He envisioned a greater number of extensive writing projects than he completed. This freeing of the self from the immediate in time, as in space, reflected in Paul's writing, is part of child—indeed, of all human—development.

Paul has enjoyed reading over his early writings, but I was the collector and preserver of them until, as a third and fourth grader, he started to save his own informational writings as reference material. A sense of the preservative value of writing developed with his sense of time: he could project both himself and his writings into the future.

Other changes in Paul's writing over time include the use of increasingly complex and differentiated structures within forms (such as more varied sections in newspapers, more complicated story plots) and conventionalizing of forms and functions (no more pieces, like his early "statements," that are unclassifiable in adult categories). As handwriting and spelling became more automatic (about third grade) he wrote faster, but did not write for longer time periods; he only produced more during a given time. As an inventive speller he had worked on writing for up to about two-hour stints.

We do not yet have comprehensive guidelines for observing growth in children's writing. Assessing mechanical errors, on the one hand, and responding subjectively to content and style, on the other, may be all that many teachers are prepared to do. They certainly have not been trained to teach writing, as Graves's survey of thirty-six universities — mainly state schools involved in teacher preparation — shows: in all he found 2 courses in the teaching of writing contrasted with 169 in reading (Graves, 1978a). Developmental patterns seen in Paul's writing include extensions in time and space as well as increasing differentiation, complexity, and conventionalizing of forms. If observations of other children bear these out or suggest other patterns, they would be measures of progress teachers could use. Instructional methods could be inferred from such a broad, developmental view of writing.

From the beginning, Paul wrote in a variety of forms for a number of different (apparent) purposes. He has written, in approximate chronological order: to name (signs), to communicate (notes), to make books or "written objects," to practice adult forms (like shopping lists and report cards), to create (stories and verse), to organize information (charts), to confirm his inner world (diary), to record and preserve information ("Know-It All" book). His spontaneous writings have been more varied than his assigned writings.

Unless teachers make room for and encourage spontaneous writing in classrooms, they have little chance to observe a child's range. School assignments may narrow rather than utilize and expand that range. Though the breadth of a child's range and the kinds of writing it contains may vary greatly from individual to individual, differentiation of forms and purposes is another measure of progress in writing. Graves (1975) has observed that young children write more when topics are self-selected rather than assigned, and when the time and duration of writing periods are flexible — conditions existing for Paul's spontaneous writings.

The knowledge and interests that are the basis for writing, by adults as by children, will reflect individual differences as well as sex and developmental status. Although Paul enjoyed writing stories and verse, his writing has been predominantly informational. When I was Paul's age, my own writing at home and at school centered on stories, poems, and descriptions of personal experiences. My hunch about sex differences in writing, as in reading, suggested by this contrast, is confirmed by Graves's research (1975). Perhaps the dominance of women among primary grade teachers has contributed to a narrowness and stereotyping of forms we expect children to write in (stories, poems, letters, personal accounts).

This study, along with other recent research in writing, indicates that observation of personal and developmental characteristics is a crucial part of the teacher's function in helping children to progress in writing when writing is viewed as a meaning-making and conveying process, not a skills exercise. Such observation might also make writing a more interesting activity for teachers and, by reflection, for their students. We speak of starting with a child "where he is," which in one sense is not to assert an educational desideratum but an inescapable fact: there is no other place the child can start from. There are only other places the teacher can start from.

Implications for Spelling

While spelling may have become a matter of habit for mature writers, *learning* to spell — as Read has argued (1971) and as this case study has documented — is largely a matter of knowledge. Spelling ability grows from understanding a system and cannot be accounted for as the product of memorized lists of unpredictably spelled words.

If learning to spell is not essentially a matter of habit, then spelling errors need not be feared as entrenching "bad habits" (wrong spellings). Paul's spelling of certain words (for example, "directions") evolved through a whole series of changes. This capacity for change — for revising one's understandings systematically — characterizes all learning, but very visibly beginning literacy learning, as will be evident again in the chapters on Paul's reading development.

Changes in Paul's spellings often resulted from his perception of differences between his spellings and those he saw in print, and from changes in his understanding of our orthography and in his consequent strategies for mastering it (for example, his shift from primarily auditory to visual spelling). Corrections did not have to come from an adult; many were made on his own. He both perceived errors independently and asked for corrections or spelling information when in doubt. Clearly *he* did not regard his spellings as fixed.

During invented spelling, Paul was transcribing speech sounds and reinventing spellings, not repeating learned word patterns. As he became concerned with spelling conventionally (obviously aware that there was one accepted spelling for each word), he seemed to monitor his spellings until he believed they were correct. A minority of them he misjudged and needed adult help to correct.

We have little information about children's judgments of their own spellings. How many misspellings are let stand because a child gives up on them rather than because he believes they are correct? How many are let stand because he knows the teacher will correct them? Graves's observations in Scottish schools (1978a) show that children given the responsibility for correcting errors in their own writing can do so. If children were not in effect relieved of correcting responsibilities by their teachers' red pencils, we might better distinguish errors committed in ignorance from those committed inattentively, and thus focus instruction appropriately.

In order to correct spelling errors themselves or with a dictionary, children must be able to generate alternative possibilities for representing sounds. Paul's practice in doing this started with invented spelling and was evident later in his attempt to enumerate all possible representations of "off," in his awareness of homonyms, in his questions about spellings when he could not decide between alternatives, and in papers where he had tried out several alternative spellings. Poor spellers I have taught, who felt defeated about arriving at correct spellings, have risen to the challenge of figuring out different ways a particular word *might* be spelled. Although the right spelling may seem arbitrary and inaccessible to them (even with dictionary in hand), this approach lets them use their reasoning and the knowledge they *do* have about spelling. With all possibilities written down before us (a group usually generates more alternatives than an individual student does), we consider which possibilities are unlikely and why, and proceed by elimination. A similar approach to teaching spelling has been described by Duckworth (1973).

As Kenneth Goodman (1969) has demonstrated so clearly for oral reading and Charles Read for invented spelling—and as Piaget revealed earlier in many contexts—children's errors are not accidental but reflect their systems of knowledge. If teachers can regard errors as sources of information for instruction rather than mistakes to be condemned and stamped out, students, as they internalize teacher responses, should be able to assume this more constructive view, too. Errors interpreted as "miscues" can help a child see and overcome the limits of his spelling strategies. For example, when Paul asked me if POST OFISS was correct, I replied, "That's the way 'office' sounds but not the way it looks." I gave him credit for the part he got right—in this case an accurate transcription—while pointing out another aspect of written English. I might also have commended him for doubling the final *s,* a new feature in his spellings which showed differentiated representation of "s" depending on its position in a word. I might also have asked him to think of another letter that could represent the "s" sound and talked about the *e* marker after the *c.*

Analysis—in contrast to counting—of children's spelling errors and consideration of changes in the nature of those errors provide a means of assessing children's spelling needs and progress. Cook (1978) has demonstrated by this kind of analysis the progress of a child who, while making the same *number* of errors on two administrations of a spelling test, made errors significantly different in *kind.* Hanna, Hodges, and Hanna (1971) have also argued for error analysis. Any structure to be developed for spelling error analysis must rest on an understanding of the nature of our orthography and of the psychology of spelling.

Through invented spelling research we have just begun to observe how some children in fact learn to spell, as distinct from our preconceptions and instructional methods. The present study—the first extensive case study of spelling development—can only suggest possible sequences to be investigated with other children.

A spelling program for kindergarten through eighth grade based on recent research into the nature of our orthography (Hanna, Hodges, and Hanna, 1971) starts with an emphasis on the alphabetic principle (sound-letter relationships), increasingly emphasizes morphology (meaning-bearing units), and finally includes context (to distinguish homonyms) and historical explanations for spellings. Paul's spelling development seems to have followed this basic sequence. The importance of meaning as an orientation to spelling was evident in his response to a spelling word I gave him as a nine-year-old: "I don't even know the word—how'm I supposed to spell it?" A remark he made the following year in response to another isolated spelling word again stressed the importance of context: "I've heard that word before. I'd know how to spell it if I could only place it." For Paul, adult-supplied information was most needed when he started spelling, to establish sound-letter correspondences; and considerably later, to reveal the historical dimension of our orthography. Morphology and context may be available through induction—not just instruction.

The point that instruction may be useful or crucial at only some stages of a learning process, and Paul's awareness of when he needed and did not need instruction, were brought home to me in a comment he made as a ten-year-old about skiing instruction: "There's a lot to learn at the start. At the stage I am now, I learn most by experimenting. Then later I can go back and learn." Surely other youngsters have a sense of how they learn and could be allowed and encouraged to take more control of their own learning. The teacher's function would then include more helping children listen to themselves and less the entire burden of diagnosing the needs of every student.

For children who start spelling through a whole word recall method rather than through figuring out sound-letter relationships, the initial steps in the sequence would be different. Some children may learn more easily from one sequence than another. Development of spelling ability may not rest on any particular sequence but on an ever-enlarging concept of spelling that increasingly approaches the actual nature of our orthography. Poor spellers even at the high school level, I have observed, have inadequate strategies for getting beyond the alphabetic principle; their errors frequently represent phonetic attempts at spellings. The more polysyllabic their vocabularies, the less adequate is this approach. They need to move on to consider morphemes and letter environments—that is, they need to consider larger units than sound-letter correspondences.

Teachers who view children's spelling errors as systematic may discover much about the learning strategies of individual children, but in order to put these insights to full use instructionally they must also view our orthography as largely systematic. In contrast to an earlier assumption that "American-English spelling is so unpredictable, the learning of each word must largely be a separate memory act" (Hanna, Hodges, and Hanna, 1971, p. 245), recent research has emphasized its predictability when letter environment and morphemic structure are taken into account (C. Chomsky, 1970; Venezky, 1970; Hanna, Hodges, and Hanna, 1971). Our spellings appear unpredictable against an expectation of consistent phoneme-grapheme correspondences at the surface level, but not if viewed as related indirectly to sound through an intermediate morphophonemic level. Our orthography preserves visually the similarity in meaning of related words (for example, muscle/muscular), which more phonemic spellings (mussle/muscular) would obscure. "By not exhibiting grapheme-phoneme correspondence, the orthography is able to reflect significant regularities which exist at a deeper level" (C. Chomsky, 1970, p. 293). Carol Chomsky contrasts two word pairs which are the same except for one vowel sound; however, the related words *look* the same: "*Nation* and *national* are not different words in the sense that *nation* and *notion* are different words" (1970, p. 289). Our orthography is a more abstract and complex system than one based on surface sound-letter correspondences, and therefore one that probably takes children longer to learn. Its advantages are for the more mature language user, especially in reading.

Good spellers appear to make use of the spelling connections among related words. Carol Chomsky has demonstrated (1970) how such relationships can be brought to children's attention in spelling instruction. Understanding such pervasive principles of our orthography must be more valuable than memorizing isolated spelling "rules" (with all their exceptions) or word lists. In the context of this view of spelling as largely systematic, asking children to memorize lists of words as the basic method in spelling instruction is inappropriate. If words lists are based on particular spelling principles, then application of those principles must be tested by asking students to spell analogous words. Memorizing lists is no guarantee of understanding. Perhaps most important of all, as Carol Chomsky has pointed out, are teachers' own assumptions about spelling, which get transmitted to their students. Are spellings things you either know or do not know because they are arbitrary (like the alphabet), or things you can be helped to figure out?

If children's learning of spelling is largely systematic, as is our orthography, then we would learn more instructionally from observing what a child knows about the system — what principles he can apply and what strategies he uses in his writings (as reflecting his *concept* of the spelling system) — than we would learn from asking what and how many words he knows. The same observations could be made of children with spelling difficulties as of those progressing normally. (In our effort to understand disabilities, perhaps we have gone too far in putting such children in a separate category with separate questions to be asked about them.) Do poor spellers spell like younger children? Or do they suffer specific deficits that yield different error patterns? As we further observe the spelling development of children, we can come to learn more about the kind of individualizing that would make spelling instruction more effective. If learning to spell is not just a function of memory, we need to explore children's understandings.

Part Two
Reading

7 Paul: Working on Reading

Prelude

Beginning reading is passage from language heard to language seen. It is a passage taken by small steps through a territory we may no longer remember.* Exactly where that passage starts is unclear. Does it start when a child "reads" faces, recognizing them and interpreting their expressions? Or when books are read aloud to him? Or when he repeats a story while turning the pages? Or not until he recognizes or decodes printed words?

Paul grew up in a home where reading was a common activity and books were everywhere. His parents enjoyed reading stories to him, which they had done regularly at bedtime since before he started to talk. He had books of his own before he

*As Clay says, "Adults find it difficult to analyse the problems of very young children as these children approach the task of learning about written language. Luria possibly provides an explanation for such difficulty. He has concluded that training and practice change the organization of the brain's activity so that the brain comes to perform an accustomed task without having to analyse this task. That is to say, the final performance of the task may be based on a network of cells in the brain which is quite different from the network that was called on originally when a performance required the help of the analytic processes" (Clay, 1975, p. 72).

could read. The only systematic instruction he received when he began reading as a preschooler was from watching "Sesame Street" and later "The Electric Company" programs.

Before Paul recognized words, he recognized stories. At two and a half years he sat down with a Curious George book that had been read aloud to him many times and, turning the pages, said the story that went with each picture. This was not a memorization of what he had heard but a kind of reconstruction. It was not simply *telling* the story because it was done in the context of looking at the book and turning the pages, saying aloud sentences that went with the pictures on each of those pages (see figure 8). To all appearances, he was reading: "He saw some pigs. He saw some pigs. Saw some other pigs. (*turn page*) They run out. (*turn page*) But Curious George had gone—gone on a cow. He had gone on a cow with the lawn mower. (*turn page*) Can't find Curious George. (*turn page*) Can't find Curious George. He had gone. (*turn page*) They took him on a truck." This corresponds to Clay's "page matching" stage (1969, p. 49), the earliest, most global attempt to find some print to match a verbal response. Only later are individual words matched to or located in print.

The first words Paul recognized were his name and "exit" (from turnpike travel). These were sight words in which presumably the total configuration—no doubt in the case of "exit" aided by the context of a green sign beside the road—stood for a word, not words perceived as phonemic representation of sounds.

working on reading (5:1-5:10)	enjoying reading (5:11-7:6)	diversified reading (7:7-9:11)
⊢—5—⊣⊢—6—⊣⊢—7—⊣		⊢—8—⊣⊢—9—⊣
(5:1-5:9) invented spelling	(5:10-7:11) toward conventional spelling	(8:0-9:8) more mature writing

Short Texts (5:1-5:7)

By the time Paul started spelling inventively (5:1), he read or recognized "cottage cheese" on a container of the same, and at his bookstore, where he had copied over the titles of his books

Now they had almost
caught up with them — but
WHERE WAS GEORGE?

Figure 8. *Page from* Curious George Gets a Medal *by H. A. Rey, published by Houghton Mifflin Company. Copyright © 1957 by H. A. Rey. Reprinted by permission.*

on a price list sheet, he was able to identify most of the titles, given quite a few seconds. Only when I asked him the price of *The Day of the Wind* did he have to pick up the book and hold it next to his list to identify it. When I asked him how he knew which word on his list said "circus," he told me "because the last letter was a *s*." Thus by the time he started spelling, Paul was using some graphic cues in reading.

The same month (5:1) he brought a book over to me and read the title, word by word, pointing to the words as he said them: "I CAN DRAW IT MYSELF BY ME." Then he took a long time to figure out the lowercase "myself" on the cover. He had asked his father to read that title to him the night before, but obviously he was not reciting from memory. He seemed aware of word boundaries in reading before he had started indicating them in his writing. This is what Clay refers to as "reading the spaces" (1969, p. 49), her final prereading language to print matching stage. Paul not only knew how to locate words in print but also seems to have known, perhaps from his own intentions as a writer (evidenced by his correcting adult misreadings of his spellings), that a printed word has one spoken equivalent.

During his first week of invented spelling, Paul made a discovery: "Once you know how to spell something, you know how to read it!" For the next few months (5:1-5:2) his main reading materials were his prolific writings. The knowledge of letter-sound correspondences that he was confirming, practicing, and developing through invented spellings was the beginning of his code breaking in reading as well.

Paul's learning to read was a less visible process than his learning to write. In the early months of code breaking, when he read everything aloud, his figuring-out processes, paradoxically, were mostly silent. Perhaps these earliest strategies—less based on sound-letter correspondences, more contextually based and diffuse—were less easily verbalized. The context he used at this time was probably largely nonverbal, such as previous knowledge of the reading material and picture clues. As his decoding skills improved, however, and he came to read more often silently, he frequently figured out words by trying alternative pronunciations aloud.

After two months of invented spelling, at 5:3, Paul's reading seemed to be based on both contextual and graphic cues. He read the title *Winnie-the-Pooh* and captions from the endpaper map: "my house," "Pooh" (though this time he started calling it "Poh," indicating use of graphic cues) "Bear's house," "Piglet's house." (He asked for "Piglet." I said, "What does *p-i-g* say?" and then he got the whole word.) He also read "Kanga's house" and "big" ("stones" I had to read for him) "and rox." "If it was a *b* instead of an *r*, it would be 'box,' " he observed, further showing his phonic skills. His misreading of "Owl's" for "Eeyore's" suggests that he was also using context cues. I had read some Pooh stories once or twice over to him, so he was moderately familiar with the characters.

A month later, with *Ape in a Cape,* which had been read aloud
to him and which provided rhyme and picture clues for some
words, Paul read "pig with a wig," "rat with a bat," "whale in a
gale"—though after deciphering "gale" correctly, he wondered
if it was right because the word was unfamiliar to him. "Toad
on" he read, then asked for "the" and slowly figured out "road."
He worked over the words very quietly to himself and only
when he had the whole phrase, said it aloud quickly: early
evidence of his not reading just word by word but attending to
meaningful word groups. In contrast to the questions he asked
during his initial invented spelling period, which were about
letters for sounds, the questions he asked about reading were
for whole words to be read for him. Thus while the letter
(sound) was the unit in writing, the word was the unit for him
in reading. Of course, he knew the sounds already.

Books were not Paul's basic reading materials, however, until he developed more fluency. At 5:3 he was still reading too
slowly and uncertainly to get much from continuous text.
When he had a book, he tended to focus on captions. For instance, in Richard Scarry's *What Do People Do All Day?*, a favorite book, he enjoyed reading little signs amid the illustrations,
such as "mail," "baggage," "hospital." He read labels, titles,
signs, and writing on commercial packages, especially cereal
boxes. Brevity may not have been the sole appeal of these
materials, which so clearly parallel Paul's writing interests at
this time (and continuing into the future). Though able to write
more sustained pieces, he again and again wrote signs and
labels and captions.

With such highly uncontrolled reading materials, Paul did
not accumulate much sight vocabulary, nor did he have particularly regular words to decode with the phonic skills evident
from his invented spelling. In reading, as in invented spelling,
almost every word was a new problem for him. This probably
made reading more difficult at the start but not, I think, in the
long run.

Barr (1974-75) observes that children using sight word
materials do not develop strategies for identifying new words
because, given the very controlled vocabulary of basals, they
never have to. Perhaps because Paul's beginning reading was

anything in print, he developed multiple strategies earlier: sight words, nonverbal and verbal context cues, and phonics. In fact, his beginning months of reading may have been largely a search for strategies in the face of the real variety and complexity of our written language. Thus his start in reading was slow, but once he consolidated these strategies, he really took off and could read almost anything by some time during his second year of reading (between six and seven years old).

During the first months of working on reading Paul seemed to be selecting print to practice his reading on; he was not just concerned with *what* the print said, but *how* it said that. Context — such as knowing the contents of the package whose label he was reading, or picture clues — limited the range of possible words, giving him some guidelines for knowing if he was right. After a few months, he was able to use sound-letter correspondences to check his readings. At 5:4, reading from the back of a cereal box, Paul said, " 'Put' — that doesn't say 'pin,' it says 'put' — 'the tail on Tony,' " comparing his expectation of "pin" (from the picture of children playing the game he had heard called "pin the tail on the donkey") with his decoding of the actual printed word. At 5:6, after reading "Magic Rocks. Grow in minutes" from one side of a box, he started on another side, which said "Grow in brilliant colors." Paul read " 'Grow in' — that's not 'minutes.' " These are early evidences of self-correction, which Clay's research (1966) indicates is a precursor to sustained reading. They also show his initial reading strategies to be more global than letter by letter decoding, at the same time that as an inventive speller he was analyzing words phoneme by phoneme. Thus Paul's earliest spelling and reading strategies differed. Only after several months of reading practice did he sometimes use phonic skills alone.

At 5:6 Paul demonstrated his ability to decode with no context cues simple words like "baby," "stop," "yes," duck," and "join" printed on cards in a reading game. His errors were nonexistent words, like "gearl" for "girl," rather than substitutions of real words. A child has no cause to pronounce nonexistent words unless his essential reading strategy is sounding out words; otherwise he will use picture, semantic, syntactic, memory, even initial letter cues to supply real word substitutions. Most of Paul's non-word errors reflected differences between his invented spelling system and standard orthography: pronunciation of *s* as invariably "s" ("iss" for "is" and "wass" for "was," which he spelled WAZ) and final *e* as "ee" ("airy" for "are" and "savvy" for "save"). "How can you tell it's silent *e*?" Paul asked after I corrected him. He was trying out alternative sounds for some letters ("fack" and then "fakey" for "face," "wahss" and then "wayss" for "was") but was without any context for judging his pronunciations.

No phonics system provides sufficient information for the accurate pronunciation of most words in English because letters frequently have more than one sound. How does a beginning reader know if *was* is "wahss," "wayss," "wass" (with the *a* pronounced as in "cat"), "wahz," "wayz," "wazz" — or "wuz"? The letters alone cannot tell him; they can at best provide alternative approximations to spoken words. The reader must then decide, on the basis of his familiarity with spoken language and the reading context, the particular word that is intended. As Frank Smith (1973) has argued, phonics is easy when you know the words, for then you know which sounds to choose. Pure decoding of English orthography, without consideration of contextual information, could produce strings of nonsense words.

At some point in learning to read, however, a child may almost abandon temporarily his use of contextual information, apparently in order to focus on a new reading strategy, as Paul seemed to be doing at 5:6. Biemiller (1970) has noted that more advanced first grade readers who are moving from using context to graphic information are less likely to make contextually appropriate substitution errors.

Although Paul did not make errors in sequencing sounds or letters in invented spellings, the same was not true in reading as he came to use sound-letter correspondences within words and not merely initial and final letters. At 5:4 he read "push out" as "push to." When I said it was not "to," he asked if it was "to" backwards. Two months later, when he was more fully into decoding, he made errors such as "clol" for "cool" and "crad" for "card." He himself was aware of the problem. "You know what sometimes happens to me when I'm reading?" he asked. "It's so difficult, I read backwards." He could later play around with his "backwardness." Looking at the word "sky," he observed that spelled backwards it was "yikes" (5:7). While this awareness guided self-corrections, errors in sequencing persisted. After reading "let" for "tell" and "nale" for "lane" (5:9), he exaggerated: "I'm reading all my words backwards today." At 5:11 he read "rails" for "liars," "flood" for "fold," and "inspycrot" for "inspector"; at 6:0 "coward" for "crowded." *R* and *l* were most susceptible to transposing to the other side of vowels, perhaps because of their vocalic quality. (Historically in English, *r* has transposed around vowels, as in Old English "bridd" to modern "bird" and Middle English "crul" to modern "curl.") That Paul made reversals in reading but not in spelling may be due to the different nature of those tasks: in invented spelling, *known* words are held in mind and *analyzed,* while in decoding, the words are *unknown* and must be *reconstructed* from letter sounds.

A little later, as Paul's spelling relied more on visual memory, sequencing errors also appeared in his writing and he produced misspellings like TIHS for "this" (at 6:1) that could never have occurred when he was sounding out spellings. Perhaps he was just stronger in auditory than visual sequencing; or he was attending more to letter *combinations* than to *sequences* in both reading and spelling at this time.

Paul's reading strategies varied not only with the level of his reading development, but also with the kind of materials he was reading. In the absence of any or of strong context cues, he let graphic miscues stand, as "ejin" for "again" in "Piglet nearly meets the Heffalump again." In the presence of strong context cues, he attended to syntactic and semantic information, as in his reading (at 5:7) of another *House at Pooh Corner* chapter title from the index:

    text: Tiggers don't climb trees.
    Paul: Tigger don't — Tiggers don't — clim trees — climb trees.

The more continuous the text, the more available are syntactic and semantic cues. In choosing noncontinuous text as his primary beginning reading material, Paul often had text that was short on internal, verbal context. Especially at the beginning of his reading, he used external and nonverbal context.

Was his choice of materials tacitly—or merely acciden-
tally—also a choice of reading strategies? It may have been that
his very concern for meaning kept him away from continuous
text at the beginning, when he read too haltingly and effortfully
at the word level to hang onto large units of meaning. Invented
spelling had given him enough phonics to help in reading, but
except when reading isolated words that precluded multiple
reading strategies, Paul used both phonics and some sort of
context—increasingly, verbal context.

Continuous Texts (5:7-5:10)

When I thought Paul was ready to read a whole book (5:6), I
suggested *Old Hat, New Hat,* one he had heard frequently but
not recently. His errors were mostly based on graphic cues; for
example, "low-see" for "loose," with the final *e* pronounced long
as in his spelling. Although I was pleased he had gone through
his first book, *he* was not particularly pleased because he had
not read it all himself; I had helped him with some words. A
month later (5:7) he was ready to try a whole book, *Go, Dog,
Go!* He read most of it aloud to himself at bedtime. Returning
to it the next morning, he ran into trouble:

> text: Where are they going?
> Paul: What are they . . .

Misreading "where" as "what," he stopped after "what are they,"
apparently sensing that "what" was wrong since the next and
last word in the sentence was "going." He was unable to figure
out "where" and after further problems with words, gave up
reading the book in frustration. But he soon tried more books.
He was working very hard on reading now with increased skill
and confidence. Picture and rhyme cues probably helped him
at 5:8 to read most of the answers in his "Electric Company"
Nitty Gritty Rhyming Riddles Book when he first got it. (I must
have read the riddles to him.) But the next day he sat down
with it for a long time—perhaps forty-five minutes—trying to
figure out every word. Unless he was sure of a word right off,
he would sound it out to himself and then say it aloud. I do
have one record of his working through a word out loud a few
months later, and perhaps something like this was going on

here. The word he was trying to figure out, in a situation where there were no context cues, was "grass"; Paul went from "jars" to "gars" to "gears" to "grass."

His new confidence about reading carried him away. A few days later, after I had read aloud several lines of a Doctor Dolittle book while he was looking on, he asked me to stop while he reread aloud what I had just done, missing only one word. He must have been following along and realized he could identify the words. Then he wanted me to go on reading the story. Reading at this time was both a great effort and a great accomplishment. A week later (5:8), as I was reading (to myself) a paperback novel, Paul leaned over my shoulder and from some distance started reading the top line of tiny print:

text: one's nerves but finally so familiar . . .
Paul: "One's never but" (made several attempts and triumphantly figured out) "finally so" (after a struggle) "family-air."

One line was enough for him—but what courage!

Paul's learning was full of surprises for me; though what appeared as its unpredictable course is, from another point of view, evidence of how little even a close and sophisticated observer sometimes knows. The following incident (5:9) may convey some of that unpredictability. It involves a game called *Talk and Take,* which is played with geometrically shaped pieces of different colors on a checkerlike board. Moves are determined by instructions on cards that each player draws and reads aloud. The game was developed as a test of syntax comprehension by Olds (1968).*

When Paul and I started playing, I read his cards for him. After a while he read some for himself but when he did not know words kept miscalling them "barbecue" and dissolving into silliness. We got perhaps a quarter through the deck of cards, leaving the game unfinished at bedtime. Though Paul had spoken of finishing it the next day, his father and I decided to put the game board away, speculating that his inability to read most of the words on the cards was so frustrating he turned to silliness.

*The game *Talk and Take* has been published by Houghton Mifflin as part of the Interaction language arts materials, J. Moffett, senior editor.

The next morning Paul said he had dreamed that his father had taken the pieces off the board. When he saw that this had in fact happened, all he expressed was the desire to play again at once. This time he started reading his own cards with no difficulty. The first one was: "Move a diamond one space, and move a square two spaces, but do not capture a piece with the square." He read fluently and followed the instructions accurately. His familiarity with the words on the cards from the day before and from their recurrences throughout the deck (controlled vocabulary) probably contributed to his reading this day. But all the decoding and reasoning required to follow the directions must have taken more concentration than Paul could sustain beyond about twenty minutes. After that (we were about a third through the deck), although he had read "picce" many times on previous cards, he could not read "pieces"; and "when," "large," and "either," which he had read earlier, he now asked me for. Finally, he asked me to read his last few cards of the game. He was no longer *practicing* reading, but *using* it for something he enjoyed. (He still loved playing this game as an eight-year-old.)

The next month (5:10) Paul read his first whole book—*Go, Dog, Go!,* which he had first attempted at 5:7. "And I only needed one word," he remarked proudly afterwards. The word he needed was "those." After I supplied it, he recognized it the next time it appeared, but the time after that he hesitated and then finally sounded it out "th-oh-ss" and then "th-oh-z," correcting according to his knowledge of real words.

Biemiller observed that beginning readers, following the phase when they increasingly used graphic information and made fewer contextually acceptable errors, increased their "ability to simultaneously use contextual and graphic information to identify words" (1970, p. 89). That the most advanced readers are making use of multiple strategies is consistent with Clay's findings (1966) that the best readers are the best self-correctors. In order to self-correct, readers must use multiple strategies—checking out phonic approximations against known words and specific context, or confirming guesses from context cues by examining graphic information.

By this time Paul had refined his phonics strategy from

sounding out on a one letter/one sound principle to applying a principle he had already used for a long time in his spelling: that one letter may have more than one sound, as in trying both "s" and "z" for the *s* in "those." That is, he could decode a printed word into several alternative pronunciations (if the first did not sound right) and then choose among them on the basis of his knowledge of the language and other contextual information. For example, "wild" he first read as "willed," then "wild," which he recognized and so decided upon; and similarly for alternative pronunciations of the *g* in "age": "ag" and "age." Obviously he was able to locate the letter susceptible to alternative sounds. For "Finn" (in Huckleberry Finn) he tried "fun," "fin"—which he did not know was correct because he was unfamiliar with the name—and then "fain." He had the same problem with the unfamiliar word "stubs," which he read correctly and then tried "stoobs." After very carefully sounding out the unfamiliar word "clad" correctly, he said, " 'Clad'—that doesn't make sense." Misreading from a spray can label "ripples cats and dogs," he asked if "ripples" was right. When I said it was "repels," he responded, "Oh, I know what that means— keeps away." Apparently he had not known what "ripples" could have meant in that context. Paul corrected his misreading of "castle," with the *t* sounded, by finally overriding graphic information through his word knowledge and the story context. Clearly, without a good oral vocabulary and a sense of what word is appropriate in a given context, phonics is of limited use. Multiple strategies seem essential for reading.

Paul's reading development so far seems broadly to have followed the same progression of strategies Biemiller (1970) observed in beginning readers: initially, a dependence on context cues; then an increasing use of graphic information and decreased use of context; and finally, after the graphic strategies are practiced, adding to them contextual strategies.

Before a child can read, must he not have some global sense of what reading is about and what it feels like? I think that was what Paul was getting from his retelling the Curious George story while looking at the appropriate illustrations and turning the pages. This very early "reading" was entirely from context. Even while he was demonstrating his "graphic" (phonic) abilities through invented spelling—which may have made him sensitive to graphic information earlier—he used context for reading. The fact that he provided me with a context clue to reading one of his first writings may indicate the usefulness of such information to him; he was trying to help me out in reading something I might have trouble with in a way he had probably found helpful. When he handed me the sheet saying PAULSKRWSH, he said something about "if you want to take the car there." Indeed, his clue did enable me to read his message before I had figured out *his* code. Later, he could use graphic information to correct his misreading, probably based on both contextual and graphic information, from a cereal box: " 'Put'—that doesn't say 'pin,' it says 'put'—'the tail on Tony' " (5:4).

As Blackie observed, "In the process of learning to read there is a sort of frontier. Once a child is over it, the main job is done. He may still need help, but he can read. He can, as teachers say, get on by himself" (Blackie, 1971, p. 58). Paul had pushed himself over the frontier; he had made his passage.

8 Other Young Readers

"A first grade classroom is by no means the only place for a child to begin reading—and maybe it is not even the best place to begin," claims Smethurst, having reviewed the literature on learning to read at home. "Throughout the five thousand years or so that people have been reading, many children have been taught to read at home. Their teachers have been parents, siblings, relatives, servants, masters, governesses, tutors, or playmates. In some societies this sort of teaching has even been commonplace. Perhaps reading is, as Margaret Mead suggests, an apprenticeship skill" (Smethurst, 1975, p. 3). Smethurst found frequent reports of children under six who learned to read outside school and documented cases of children five and younger taught by nonprofessional teachers. These early readers did not learn by any one method. Some learned informally, selecting from their environment what they needed for reading. Others learned through direct teaching, either by a code emphasis or a meaning emphasis approach.

Through case studies we can see the range of ways in which children learn to read. The classroom case studies being gathered by the Educational Testing Service for their Collaborative Research Project on Reading indicate the diversity and individuality among beginning readers in the primary grades. However, most of the few published case studies of non-problem readers have been of children who learned to read before school. Durkin's study (1966) of children who read early revealed wide individual differences among the children but some common patterns in home environment and responsiveness. Clark's research on young fluent readers in Scotland, published ten years later, confirmed Durkin's findings and stressed the diverse patterns in the abilities, interests, and backgrounds of the children — findings she hoped would "lead to greater caution in assuming that certain strengths are essential prerequisites for success in reading — or equally important, that particular weaknesses inevitably lead to failure" (Clark, 1976, p. x).

Torrey describes an "unlikely" self-taught early reader — a child who, on the basis of currently accepted indicators of reading success, might have been predicted to fail: "John has no more than average tested verbal ability and perhaps even less than average cultural stimulation in the direction of reading. The key factor in reading therefore must be something else. Large vocabulary, sophisticated thinking, accurate articulation of standard English, active encouragement and instruction in reading skills, may very well help a child learn to read. However, even a single case like John's shows us that they are not indispensable, that is, that neither success nor failure in reading can be predicted in individual cases from these factors alone" (Torrey, 1973, p. 156). While Durkin saw home environment and attitude as important to early reading, Torrey points to this child's ability as a learner: "He appears to have asked just the right questions in his own mind about the relation between language and print and thus to have been able to bridge the gap between his own language and the printed form" (1973, p. 157). John's case suggests that intelligence (as measured by standard tests) is not the critical difference between children who construct the rules of beginning reading for themselves and those who are instructed.

Theoretical research has tended toward a constructionist view of reading, in contrast to what might be called the "instructionist" view usually taken by educational research. In the instructionist view, the locus of organizing and generalizing knowledge is in the teacher; in the constructionist view, it is within the learner. The "truth" perhaps will be found to vary widely among beginning readers, some virtually teaching themselves while others depend more on instruction.

Other case studies challenge the commonly accepted notion that oral language acquisition must precede learning to read. Steinberg and Steinberg (1975) taught their son to identify letters and words before he could speak. Since learning to read is generally equated with being taught to read in school, "readiness," the Steinbergs argue, means readiness for formal instruction in a school setting, not necessarily readiness to begin the process of reading in itself.

Söderbergh (1971) started from a hypothesis about the similarity of language and literacy learning: "Now if a child learns to talk at a certain age without formal instruction, solely by being exposed to language, and if written language is to be considered as an independent system, why cannot a child learn to read *at the same age and in the same way* as he is learning to talk, solely by being exposed to written language? He would then be supposed to attack the written material, forming hypotheses, building models, all by himself discovering the code of the written language" (Söderbergh, 1971, pp. 15-16). Söderbergh's study documents this process in detail, revealing a child's spontaneous induction of word analysis — first morphemes, then phonemes — from words learned by sight. Studies of child language development as well as invented spelling have revealed children's ability to abstract principles about language. It has become increasingly clear that language acquisition is not merely imitative but systematic and creative, in the sense of the child constructing the rules for himself. A striking example is children's regularizing of irregular verbs ("goed," "hurted") once they have mastered the rule of past tense formation.

From studies of individual preschool children Harste, Burke, and Woodward argue the similarity between literacy learning and oral language development. They found that preschool children had discovered much about print before formal language instruction: "Included in the child's model of reading and writing . . . was a functional expectation for print, an expectation for how language operates in alternate contexts, and a growing control of English orthography, wordness, left-to-right and top-to-bottom directionality, grapheme-phoneme correspondence and syntax" (Harste, Burke, and Woodward, forthcoming). Learning to read, in a literate environment, starts long before teaching to read.

Case studies widen the parameters within which we view learning to read. They remind us that the methods and time schedules by which these skills are conventionally taught are not necessarily conditions for learning them. "Certain characteristics may appear crucial because of the particular approach used in learning to read and the fact that learning to read normally takes place in a group situation — in school" (Clark, 1976, p. ix).

As learning processes exist in their wholeness only in individuals, only through studying individuals may we see these processes at work. And only through close and empathetic observation of individual human beings may we know the unmeasurable efforts of will, the frustrations and triumphs of learning, which make it finally worthwhile and enduring. Learning to read and to write, to understand how printed language works, is not easy. Paul learned to write and read earlier than some, not because these tasks were easy for him but because they were possible and because he commited himself to the great effort of learning them.

9 Paul: Enjoying Reading

Toward Silent Reading (5:11-6:10)

One indication that Paul was over the hump — beyond the hard-working-at stage — in reading was his working hard at mathematics (6:0). His concentration, his frustration at errors and interruptions while mentally adding numbers recalled his early invented spelling behavior. In developing his own three Rs curriculum, he seemed to balance out his learning in such a way that he was working hard at initial skills in only one particular area at a time: periods of intense effort on spelling alternated with periods of intense effort in reading, and times of concentrated work on mathematics were interspersed between these. His schedule was very different from a conventional first grade day of short time periods for each of the Rs. Paul worked in spurts, a characteristic that Durkin (1966) noted among her early readers.

Paul's "working on reading" period corresponds to the first of Chall's (1979) reading stages, decoding or learning to read; and her second stage, reading for fluency, is what I have called "enjoying reading." Both fluency and enjoyment are evident in Paul's comment (6:1): "I really like to read — little, simple things." The new quality that he articulated was enjoyment. Again, at 6:7, he said, "I just love reading."

Several other changes were clearly observable: the beginning of silent reading, an increase in reading speed and associated changes in reading strategies, an eagerness to try reading anything in print, and rereading of familiar books.

Just before his sixth birthday, Paul made a spontaneous shift to silent reading, in the back seat of the car on our way home from the library with *Yertle the Turtle* by Dr. Seuss. Unsure what the silence while he looked at the book indicated, I asked Paul the next day whether he had been reading the words or the pictures. "The words!" he answered, piqued at my stupidity. "There's nothing else to read."

He often moved his lips while reading to himself so it was not yet truly visual reading, but it was reading for and to himself. I interpreted the silence as meaning that he no longer needed to have the accuracy of his reading confirmed (or corrected) by a listening adult, that he was ready to be his own monitor. Paul's view — explained to me when he was nine years old — was that he read aloud because *he* needed to hear himself in order to know if his reading was correct. Because I assumed for Paul an adult distinction between silent speech for oneself and out loud speech for others, I overlooked the possibility that he could be reading aloud for himself, as I sometimes also overlooked the egocentric function of his speech when he encountered difficulties in an activity and was expressing his frustration rather than (as I responded) asking for help. According to Vygotsky (1962), inner speech develops — egocentric speech becomes internalized — by about age seven. At this point (6:10) all of Paul's reading was silent, except when he specifically wanted to share the *content* of what he was reading. This development parallels Vygotsky's sequence for speech, with speech for oneself (egocentric) distinguished from speech for others (social) first through function — being intended for oneself although spoken aloud — and later also through form — silent, internalized speech. Thus Paul's movement toward silent reading can be seen as part of his growth in internalized thought.

Quite often, as a six-year-old, Paul still chose to read aloud. One evening he read aloud to me two familiar books: *Old Hat, New Hat* by S. and J. Berenstain, and *The Cat in the Hat Comes*

Back by Dr. Seuss, both first grade level.* Since it was late in
the evening and he was tired, the less intense effort required for
reading now was obvious. He read *Old Hat, New Hat* with only
one error; the very few errors he made on *The Cat in the Hat
Comes Back* were largely self-corrected when a phrase did not
sound right to him. He got into trouble once by disregarding a
period, and several words later he was puzzled. I think his in-
tonations were based not on printed punctuation but on syntax
and meaning, and perhaps recall of hearing a story read aloud
before. Once beyond the halting, working-on-reading phase,
Paul read aloud with great expression — another aspect of his
enjoying reading. I have wondered, hearing some other begin-
ners reading very flatly, whether and how they were read aloud
to. Would Paul have read with such expression and intonation
if he had not been read to that way — if he did not have that
sound of reading in his head?

Very slow reading threatens coherence. I suppose Paul chose
short texts when he first started reading partly to avoid loss of
meaning. (The longest texts he read then were his own
writings, whose meanings he must already have had in mind.)
Increased speed and accuracy enabled him to tackle continuous
text and then to shift to silent reading for meaning. I have no
record of Paul's oral reading speed during his first year and a
half of reading, but it was labored and halting. During the
following year it was becoming fluent; at 6:6 he read a familiar
Curious George book (second grade level) at 100 words per
minute, and at 6:9 an unfamiliar Shel Silverstein poem (fourth
grade level) at 110 words per minute. I doubt that his silent
reading was faster than his oral reading at this point. Almost a
year later, it was faster, but by then the two kinds of reading
were more fully differentiated. While he was still moving
toward silent reading as a norm and still using oral reading for
feedback on accuracy and not entirely to share material, I imagine the processes were much the same in nature and speed.

The increase in Paul's reading speed was not merely

---

*Reading levels of all materials below fourth grade level have been deter-
mined by the Spache formula, and of materials at higher levels by the Dale-
Chall formula.

associated with greater speed and accuracy in word identification, but also with changes in strategy, which in turn reflected a changed approach to reading. With more difficult material, Paul made more word substitution errors and often let these go by even if they did not make sense, in the interest of getting ahead, in the pursuit of understanding some unit larger than the word or perhaps even the sentence. "Coward beach" was let stand for "crowded beach," and "common ground" for "cinnamon ground." Sometimes, after reading to the end of a sentence, he made corrections, as in this instance (6:1):

> text: Yes, I pressed the silent alarm button.
> Paul: Yes, I pressed the s ——— army button — silent alarm.

A few days before this, while I was reading, he had picked up one of my books (John Hay's *In Defense of Nature*) and had read a whole page silently. Later Paul explained that he had read the words he knew and skipped or said something he realized was inaccurate for the hard words. His substitutions, based on graphic and phonic cues, served as place holders.

Paul's strategies for deciphering individual words depended on the length and structure of the word as well as the available context. "Rules for pronouncing English monosyllables are relatively simple; those for pronouncing polysyllabic but monomorphemic words are more complex; and those for polymorphemic words, the most complex" (Venezky, 1970, p. 121). As Paul selected increasingly difficult reading materials, he was confronted by more polysyllabic and polymorphemic words. His unit for decoding such words was not sound-letter correspondences but morphemes; he was appropriately dealing with chunks, not single letters. His errors reflected substitution or distortion of morphemes: "amazement" for "assortment" (6:0), and asking me whether "environment" was "evement" or "erment" (6:11). When aided by context he was often able to decipher polymorphemic words, as "not designed for recharging" on a label (6:1). Compound words, which are less complex, were easier for him: "tenderfoot," "backward," and "fingerprints" he read correctly the same month.

An extreme example of an isolated word without context for Paul was "Grand Pré" spelled out in flower beds on a lawn in that unfamiliar location. The letters were so large that the whole word could not be encompassed visually from the close range where Paul was attempting to read it. After saying the letters correctly, one by one, he pronounced "grand." I suppose because there was no context to confirm this reading, he made further attempts which illustrate his handling of phonics in monomorphemic words: "garnd" and "jarnd." Paul knew that there were alternative sounds for some letters, so he experimented with these when his first choice produced a word unacceptable to him. He had little knowledge yet of environmental constraints on vowel and some consonant sounds. In other instances, when "ag" sounded wrong he tried "age"; he tried "kinnamon" and then "cinnamon"; "stubs," read correctly, was an unfamiliar word so he tried "stoobs." Recognizability and contextual sense were his guides to correctness rather than complex phonic rules.

The importance of context as a supplement to phonics is evident in the following instances. Paul (6:0) was reading a sign at the U.S. customs station on the Canadian border: "What's that?—'mahter'? 'All drivers turn off mahter'—oh, 'motor'!" The "maht" pronunciation of "mot-" is understandable by analogy with common words like "not" and "hot." On a Pop Tarts box he read "tuck in your pocket" correctly, but the unfamiliar "Friar Tuck" came out as "fair truck" (6:2).

Beyond this period of moving toward silent reading, Paul's information about words (for instance, his store of familiar morphemes) would increase, and he would become more aware of environmental constraints on letter sounds and more aware of morphophonemic and stress changes in polymorphemic words; but his basic reading strategies were established. He used letter-sound correspondences, morphemes, and semanti_ and syntactic context for reading.

The diversity of his strategies accompanied the variety in his selection of reading materials during this period. Anything in print was potential reading matter for Paul: selections from adult books, signs and labels, new and harder story books, old familiar stories, and new easy books for rapid reading. His purposes, too, seemed more diverse: practicing decoding on harder materials, gaining speed on easy materials and expressiveness in reading aloud familiar books, enjoying the content of stories and the sounds of poems as he read them.

The reading materials he selected did not, like a basal series, show a neat progression in difficulty. There were plateaus, regressions, and abrupt advances in level—not surprisingly, given the several dimensions or purposes of his reading. He might on the same day attempt adult material and read an easy book. During this period of movement toward silent reading, his choice of materials showed more variety than was true during his previous year and a half of beginning reading. Reading levels ranged from pre-primer through fifth to sixth grade, not including the scattered adult material.

Although at school he was given individual work in informational texts on nature and history, he did not seek out informational reading on his own for another year. His reading of signs and labels, though superficially informational, did not involve the gathering of facts, later repeated or used, which characterized his subsequent informational reading. He seemed to read signs and labels at least in part to practice reading. What he liked to gather at this time were jokes and riddles rather than facts. He eagerly read books containing them and later retold the jokes or asked the riddles, so that functionally this resembled reading for information. The joke and riddle books were resource or reference works to which he went to gather as well as enjoy a particular kind of material that he could store for future use.

Paul gained fluency and expressiveness by rereading favorite books—some of them books that had been read aloud to him before he could read. This kind of practice, which seemed important for both his enjoyment and his mastery of reading, is often not provided in school. Basal readers repeat words but not stories, which is quite a different thing and does not give practice with broader language structures or the satisfaction of having read challenging material really well.

By far the greatest number of transcripts and tape recordings of Paul's reading that I collected are from this period. Later, his reading aloud was too infrequent; earlier, notations of his reading short texts had sufficed, and as he began on continuous texts I think I had not wanted to intrude on his still effortful practicing. He knew when I was taping a reading and felt comfortable with it — even enjoyed performing — when his reading became more fluent.

The first transcript is of Paul reading from *The Wump World,* a book that had been read aloud to him several times over the previous year or so. This familiarity probably helped him with some words, especially names like "Pollutians"; but I could see that he was reading it all — concentrating on the words and on keeping his place without a finger on the fairly long and finely printed lines. It was not easy reading for him but he kept right along. The author's dedication, which he started with, had not been read to him. In these transcripts, Paul's deviations from the text are given in parentheses.

> For my wife Margaret who appreciates (*What?!* [*I supplied the word]*) the marvels (*marvelous*) of nature as much as anyone.
>
> The Wump World was a small world, very much smaller than our world. There were no great oceans, lofty (*softly*) mountains, giant forests, or broad sandy deserts. The Wump World was mostly grassy meadows and clumps of leafy green trees with a few winding rivers and lakes. But it was perfect for the Wumps, who were the only creatures living there.
>
> The Wumps were simple grass-eaters and spent most of their time grazing on the tall tender grass that grew in the meadows. In warm weather they cooled themselves in the crystal-clear (*crystal . . . criestal*) rivers and lakes. And at night they slept in the shelter of the bumbershoot trees to keep the dew off their backs . . .
>
> As the monsters swooped down to land, huge (*hudge . . . huge*) legs sprang from their bulging sides, and like gaping (*japing*) mouths doors flew open, then ramps shot to the ground. And down the ramps came a horde of tiny creatures swarming out onto the meadow.
>
> These were the Pollutians from the planet Pollutus . . . *

"Lofty," "gaping," and apparently "crystal" were unfamiliar words; after saying "crystal" correctly, Paul looked at the word again, no doubt observing the "cry." "Hudge" he corrected to

*From B. Peet, *The Wump World* (Boston: Houghton Mifflin, 1970), pp. 1-6. (Fifth to sixth grade level.)

"huge" after looking at the accompanying picture. "Marvelous," which he let stand for "marvels," perhaps carried its meaning as well in that form.

Another reading during this same month (6:3) was of a text unfamiliar to Paul, a book called *Estimation,* which I had gotten for him because of his interest in numbers. He did not, however, continue to read the book on his own. In contrast to his usual oral reading, he often either ignored punctuation or at least minimized intonation here—perhaps because he had not heard it read aloud before, or because he needed to concentrate on getting the words, or because it was not dramatic or a book he really enjoyed. His most expressive readings were of favorite books he had read aloud several times, like *Bert's Hall of Great Inventions* (a "Sesame Street" book) in which he really hammered up the dialogue.

> But if I asked you, "How high is the church nearest your home?" you probably could not measure it. You would have to guess—or estimate—how high it is.
>
> An estimate (*éstimàte*) is a careful guess. Many times, an estimate (*éstimàte*) is good enough as an answer to such questions as "How many?" or "How high?" or "How far?" Of course your estimate (*éstimàte*) must be a good one if your answer is to be helpful. Most people need a little practice to be good estimators.
>
> Let's do some experiments . . . *

Paul's misstressing "estimate" is not technically a reading error. Stress in English must always be supplied by the reader on the basis of his knowledge of the language. With monosyllabic words—the basic vocabulary of beginning reading texts—there is no problem of stress, but with words more lengthy and complex in structure, the reader is constantly supplying stress. (Some older children with severe reading difficulties do not accurately do this and so fail to recognize words they have otherwise sounded out correctly.)

Stress shifts within the same base word because of affixation ("lócate" and "locátion") or function ("éstimate," noun; "éstimàte," verb) are predictable in English, but were among

---

*C.F. Linn, *Estimation* (New York: Crowell, 1972). (Second grade level.)

the latest rules Paul learned about language. At 7:3 he spoke of "ignórance" (stressed like "ignore") and at 7:4 "phótogràphy" (like "photograph"), a word he had earlier seen in print. He continued to stress some words according to their most familiar form rather than the stress shift rules of affixation at 7:8 — "I've done a lot of récording." However, he was aware though uncertain of stress shift, for in that same month, after talking about the sewing maching being "perfécted" since Betsy Ross's time, he added, "If that's how you say it." When I asked him how else it might be said, he replied "pérfected." Such misstresses apparently did not arise just from visual recognition of the familiar form of a word — that is, from reading — for Paul also said "pronóunciation" instead of "pronunciation," emphasizing its base in "pronounce." This grasp of the lexical base of related words aided Paul's spelling and vocabulary development, and probably his reading comprehension as well. "Antícipàtory," a reading he made at 7:9, was probably an error in the service of comprehension.

Paul was sensitive to intonation patterns that disrupted meaning, and he generally corrected these when he read aloud. The following excerpt from his taped reading (at 6:6) of *Curious George Goes to the Hospital,* a familiar book, indicates his dependence on syntax and meaning rather than punctuation marks for his intonation. Both Weber (1970) and Clay (1972), in analyzing miscues of beginning readers, found children making significant use of syntactic cues and not just decoding word by word. Self-corrections characterized the most proficient beginning readers. "The courage to make mistakes, the 'ear' to recognize that an error has occurred, the patience to search for confirmation — these were the characteristics of children who made good progress in their first year of reading" (Clay, 1972, p. 119).

> What could be in it? George could not resist. (*What could it — what could be in it George could — what could be in it? George could not re-sist.*) . . .
>
> The next morning George did not feel well. He had a tummy-ache and did not want to eat his breakfast.
>
> The man was worried. He went to the telephone and called Doctor Baker. "I'll be over as soon as I can," said the doctor . . .

The man sat with him for a while. "Now I have to leave you, George," he finally said. "I'll be back first thing in the morning before they take you to the operating room. Nurse Carol will tuck you in when it's time to sleep."

Then he left. George just sat there and cried. (*Then he left George just — left George, just sat there and cried. — left. George just sat there and cried.*)*

Three months later (6:9) I recorded Paul reading from a new book, *Where the Sidewalk Ends.* Although he had not seen or heard these poems before, he read fluently (110 words per minute on the example given below) and with expression and enjoyment. He corrected most errors that disturbed the sense or rhythm.

One Inch Tall

If you were only one inch tall, you'd ride a worm to school.
The teardrop of (*teardrop off . . . the teardrop of*) a crying ant
    would be your swimming pool.
A (*The*) crumb of cake would be a feast
And last you seven days at least,
A flea would be a frightening beast
If you were one inch tall.

If you were only one inch tall, you'd walk beneath the door,
And it would take about a month to get down to the store.
A bit of fluff would be your bed,
You'd swing upon a spider's thread,
And wear a thimble (*the thi . . . a thimble*) on your head
If you were (*only*) one inch tall.

You'd surf across the kitchen sink upon a stick of gum.
You couldn't hug your mama, you'd just (*cause you'd*) have to
    hug her thumb.
You'd run from people's feet in (*— from people's feet in* [repeated])
    fright,
To move a pen would take all night,
(This poem took fourteen years to write —
'Cause I'm just (*only . . . I'm just*) one inch tall).†

*From M. and H. A. Rey, *Curious George Goes to the Hospital* (New York: Scholastic, 1966). (Second grade level.)
†"One Inch Tall" from *Where the Sidewalk Ends: The Poems and Drawings of Shel Silverstein.* © 1974 by Shel Silverstein. By permission of Harper and Row, Publishers, Inc.

A month later (6:10) at bedtime, as I was sitting beside Paul's bed, he started to read aloud another poem from *Where the Sidewalk Ends* but after the first line decided to read it silently — a decision he made about almost all his reading from this point on.

During most of this period Paul was in first grade (6:1-6:11), yet I have said remarkably little about his reading at school. Since he read more extensively and in more difficult books at home where I also could observe him directly, this leading edge of his reading development has been the focus of this chapter. His first grade teacher, appreciating that Paul could already read, placed him in more advanced basals (upper first and second grade levels) and gave him supplementary material. In a school setting he did not work with the concentration he showed at home, and throughout the years of this study all his teachers commented on his inefficient use of time and slowness in completing usually workbook assignments.

Paul's writings outside of school suggest that had he been asked to produce workbooks rather than consume them, he might have attended more to the task. His first grade teacher, observing how Paul lit up one day when I came into the classroom, felt that he depended on my responsiveness for motivation. Since he already knew how to read and write, he may have viewed what he had to learn in first grade quite differently. Three years afterward, what he recalled learning about reading and writing were skills and tests in the workbooks and new words in writing. Silent reading was his own accomplishment: "I taught myself how to read in my head. I remember a lot of the kids couldn't do it."

Silent Reading, Longer Texts (6:11-7:6)

The period from 6:11 to 7:6 was transitional, encompassing Paul's completed move into silent reading and the beginning of his next development, informational reading.

Paul no longer asked his parents to read aloud to him, though he enjoyed his second grade teacher's reading the Narnia books aloud to the class. In independent reading he advanced from books that were short stories, like the Dr. Seuss books, to novels like *The Phantom Tollbooth* (fifth to sixth grade level), which I had actually bought to read aloud to him. Though he had previously read some equally difficult material, it had not been so lengthy; short stories he could read through in one sitting, but novels had to be sustained over days and days. This move to longer texts was supported at school by the availability of novels (Paul mentioned *The Wind in the Willows* and the Dr. Dolittle books) and a daily silent reading time.

As a second grader, Paul may have done more reading at school than at home. Our family had moved, for this academic year, to Cambridge, Massachusetts. With many friends within walking distance, Paul's time was more taken up with social activities than in the country—hence less reading at home. At school he was in a combined second and third grade classroom where much time was devoted to reading both text and trade books. Paul went through several basals (second to fourth grade levels) and their accompanying workbooks as well as the books he chose for silent reading.

The main source of errors in Paul's reading from this time onward was unfamiliar words, such as "magenta," which he assimilated to a similar but more familiar word and pronounced "magneta," and "eider," which he pronounced "eeder" in accord with his pronunciation of "either." Proper names like "Flaherty" and "Uranus" were more troublesome and less accurately rendered. Only familiarity with a wider range of words could improve his reading technically.

While his reading at home was often "recreational"—comics, *Mad* magazine, and Tintin books—Paul was also getting into another kind of reading. One evening, while choosing his bedtime reading, he said, "Things like dictionaries and almanacs settle my mind. I have two dictionaries and one almanac" (7:4). His growing interest in informational reading marks the next period in Paul's reading development.

Before he fully moved into that period, and perhaps as preparation for it, Paul became very concerned with word meanings. Knowledge of vocabulary is often more crucial for comprehension of informational than of fictional material. The story of Paul's working on vocabulary—at least that small part of it made visible through his explicit comments and questions—is told in the next section.

10 Paul: Working on Vocabulary

Most of Paul's questions and comments on vocabulary that I recorded are from the latter part of the transitional period in reading just presented and from the early months of the next period. An earlier and briefer clustering of comments and questions on specific word meanings occurred at 5:3, when he had asked about or produced explanations for certain names, like "ice cream," "Cheerios," and "silverware." Almost all of these words referred to concrete objects and were compounds of fairly common English words. Paul assumed a direct and logical reason for the names: "That's why it's called 'ice cream'—because it's cream made into ice."

His later curiosity about vocabulary shows a more sophisticated awareness of morphemes and word derivations. Since both of his parents enjoyed words and were knowledgeable about derivations, it is not surprising that Paul picked this up; the timing, however, was a matter of his own development. This sophistication is already evident in a speculation he made at 6:10 during our first electrical storm of the season. Paul was saying how he used to think thunder and lightning were the same thing, but now he knew thunder was the noise and lightning the light. Then he speculated that "thunder" came from two words in a different language: "thun" meaning *noise* and "der" meaning *loud*. Paul also makes explicit here the processes of differentiation and increasing context independence that shape vocabulary learning as well as other forms of cognitive growth.

More frequently than context dependence through an event, such as the storm linking "thunder" and "lightning" in meaning, I noted verbal context dependence. Paul learned to use new words accurately in established phrases or verbal contexts, so it was often some time before the limits to his knowledge of word meaning—in contrast to word usage—were evident. When I asked Paul what "conquer" meant (7:3), he said, "Like fight—like 'The Martians are going to conquer the world.' " When I asked him whether he knew it meant that you *won* the fight, he said he did not, and then amended his earlier statement to "Earth is going to conquer the Martians." Although Paul had used "disintegrate" appropriately in conversation with a friend, a few days later (7:3) when I used the word to help define "demolish" for Paul, he asked what "disintegrate" meant. Thus he seemed to acquire some words as meanings in contexts and have a better sense of their usage than their isolated meanings.

For other words, however, he showed a clearer sense of meaning than usage. Talking about the windup mechanism on a child's record player, he said (7:4), "It avoids you from making it go too fast." Having drawn a picture on a soft sheet of cardboard that was indented ("etched" Paul called it) from the pencil pressure, he remarked, "I have to transpose it onto paper" (7:3). A moment later he added, "I'm not going to copy it," by way, I assume, of explaining "transpose," which here meant to make a crayon rubbing—quite literally to place (pose) the picture across (trans) onto the paper. At 8:6 he remarked, "At first it pondered me why nine wasn't prime" (a prime number), using "ponder" syntactically like "puzzle." Paul did not acquire both word meaning and appropriate usage at the same time.

Although he generally skimmed over unfamiliar words while reading continuous text—in the interest, I suppose, of maintaining continuity while wresting what meaning he could from context—he frequently asked about unfamiliar words he heard or he read in short texts. On the cover of a booklet of colored plastic sheets that his father had given him was the word "poly-chrome." Paul asked what "poly" meant (7:2), correctly seg-menting the morpheme. His father answered that it meant "many" and that "polychrome" meant "many-colored." "Then 'chrome' means 'color,' " said Paul, establishing the second morpheme. He had defined "priceless" (on the Stanford-Binet vocabulary test at 7:3) as "not worth anything"; but a few weeks later, after coming upon "priceless" in something he was reading, asked what it meant. I explained that it referred to something worth so much you could not buy it. Several days later, when I was telling him about some shoelaces I had gotten for his sneakers, hoping they were the right length since you couldn't buy the kind that originally came with the shoes, Paul said, "They're priceless shoelaces." He remembered only part of my verbal definition (that you can't buy it) but was characteris-tically eager to *use* the new word.

Paul was very actively working on vocabulary, not just "ab-sorbing" it from a verbal environment (if it can be passively ab-sorbed). After asking about a word meaning, he sometimes im-mediately tested his understanding by using it in new contexts. For instance, at 7:8 he asked the meaning of "synchro-nize"—like 'synchronize your watches,' " he explained, already using it correctly in a conventional context. I defined it in terms of all the clocks in the house saying exactly the same time at once. Paul then asked about "singing together" as an instance, and a few minutes later tried extending the meaning of "syn-chronize" to a more remote context. "Daddy, I can make a sentence with 'synchronize': I synchronize my television with 'Hogan's Heroes.' " He seemed to be testing his grasp of the concept—the relationship expressed—by applying it to dif-ferent situations.

Another kind of application of new knowledge about words—this time about a prefix—is evident in a second inci-dent at 7:8. The word "yesteryear" at first puzzled Paul, but then he realized he could figure out what it meant: "Oh yeah, like 'yesterday'—yesteryear, yestercentury." In writing, speak-ing, and especially reading, Paul was dealing with a greater proportion of polymorphemic words, and part of his work on vocabulary was learning the meanings of more bound morphemes. While watching a television commercial that probably used the word "stimulate," Paul asked (7:4), "What does 'stimu' mean, anyway—like stimu-late, Stimu-dent?" And at 8:3 he asked what "sub" meant—"like 'subconscious,' 'suburban,' 'submarine'? Does it mean 'under'?" I asked him if he had studied word parts like "sub" in school, and he said he had not. When I asked him how he guessed "sub" meant "under," he said he was thinking of "submarine." (It came out later in a discussion that he thought "suburban" meant very hot, like a desert. We agreed that he had probably confused it with "Sahara.") He had asked several days before about "subconscious"—about how your subconscious mind works.

Paul's morphemic awareness was also apparent in his invention of words. At 7:5 he reported inventing a new word, "mannérily—like it's mannérily to say please and thank you." (Note the stress shift from "mánner" to "mannérily.") His definition was expanded through further examples of the word in sentences—applied to different situations. (I am sure he was not familiar with "mannerly.") He coined other words by analogy: "grossening," used analogously to "sickening" in "to be grossening" and "to taste grossening" (7:5). At 7:7 he told me "an equation in numerétical order," which he said was like alphabetical order: 1 + 2 = 3. After he had gotten a chemistry set which introduced him to a new vocabulary, he made up chemical names (8:3): SODIUM RICECOLI (pronounced as in lico*rice*), SODIUM INCODATE, SODIUM IMBOTATE. The same month he opened ALOKO'S RESTURAUNT, whose menu featured PRETSCUIT (pretzel-Triscuit), PEAT-SEL (peanut butter on pretzel), and TREANUT SAND-WICH (Triscuit with peanut butter). Paul recalled (8:6) his father asking him long ago whether, if he came to a word he didn't know in reading and figured how to sound it out, he would know what it meant. He had said "no," but added now "unless it contained some old Greek words I knew." (I had recently been analyzing Greek and Latin derivatives in some texts.) When I asked him what old Greek words he knew (none that I was aware of), he said, by way of example, if the word was "arctical" he would know it had something to do with very cold ("arctic").

He seemed to assume that words not only have referents but also etymological or derivational meanings. When he asked about "rodents" (8:3), he asked not only if they were animals like squirrels but what "rodent" *meant.* Paul suggested it might mean "little runner."

As a seven-year-old he was clearly aware of multiple meanings for words and enjoyed punning with his friends. At the dinner table one night (7:5) after a discussion about rare lamb, he commented: "There's two kinds of rare. Like rare, it's hard to find: a red and gold and silver (etc.) diamond is hard to find. And like 'Is your meat too rare?' " His responses to some Stanford-Binet vocabulary items show a continuing growth in his facility with multiple meanings:

Definition of "straw"
  7:3   "A thing you suck through to drink milk or orange juice."
  9:5   "Made of paper or plastic, and you drink through it. Or it's sort of a grain—a wheat kind."
Definition of "tap"
  7:3   "Which kind? Like tap your finger or a water tap?" (He proceeded to explain how a water tap worked.)
  9:5   "To hit lightly (he demonstrated) or (he imitated tap dancing). It's also a water spout or faucet."

His ninth birthday was on a Sunday and he pointed out the pun: son-day.

At 8:6 he looked up words in the dictionary to see how many different meanings they had. Then he compared the number he found in his Thorndike-Barnhart Junior Dictionary with the number in his father's paperback Merriam-Webster. In line with the way he defined words himself, Paul preferred the illustrative use of words in sentences in his dictionary to the synonym-type definitions in his father's.

As a five-year-old Paul had asked about the reason for certain familiar names like "silverware" and "hamburger," but as a seven- and eight-year-old he was actively seeking out the meanings of unfamiliar words and then using those words in his talk. His questions and comments about word meanings were more sophisticated, reflecting new levels of awareness about morphemes and derivations. He was resourceful in figuring out meanings from his knowledge of word parts, and he explored multiple meanings through usages he heard and read as well as through his dictionary. His greater awareness and precision about word meanings seem directly related to his move into informational reading.

11 Paul: Diversified Reading

"Reading" was no longer the unitary kind of process it had seemed when Paul was learning to read and later gaining fluency. In contrast to his beginning-to-end immersion in fictional works, he read selectively in informational texts and could skim for specific information. The period I call "diversified reading" Chall (1979) calls "reading for learning the new," which was certainly one of its hallmarks for Paul, too. I have focused instead on his development of diversified reading strategies, resulting from informational reading becoming a major—if not *the* major—aspect of Paul's reading repertoire. Since a differentiated approach to reading, varying according to the demands of the material and the purposes of the reader, characterizes proficient adult reading, it does not help to distinguish this period in Paul's reading from whatever the next one will be (9:11 is merely a cutoff point somewhere in the midst of the period I have called "diversified reading," not its termination).

Informational Reading

Paul's emphasis now was no longer on mastering the mechanics of reading but on the content. Most of his errors were caused by limits in his word knowledge, as became particularly apparent when he tackled scientific, historical, and other "subject area" texts with their specialized vocabularies. Had his parents been chemists and chemical terms familiar to his ears, Paul probably would not have misread "talcum" as "talsum" or "bisulphate" as "bulfate" on his chemistry set (7:7). Familiar geographical names he read correctly and he erred on unfamiliar ones. "Prussia" he read as "Prussa," although a while earlier he had read "Asia" correctly — a word that might well be problematic for a young reader to sound out, syllabify, and stress. "Oregon" came out as "ór-gee-on" and "Morocco" as "móre-uh-ko". Unless he had already heard of the Loch Ness monster, I doubt that he would have pronounced "Loch" correctly as he did.

Paul's reading material often included words unfamiliar to him. That he was learning vocabulary from his reading became apparent with words he mispronounced but used correctly in terms of their meaning in conversation, like "ál-bin-oh" for "albino" and "dée-suh-bulz" for "decibels" at 8:8.

His reading *The I Hate Mathematics! Book* by Marilyn Burns (7:7), soon followed by the dictionary and *The Guinness Book of World Records,* marks Paul's turn toward informational reading — a turn foreshadowed in his prereading days by frequent requests to hear Richard Scarry's *What Do People Do All Day?, Busy, Busy World,* and *The Best Word Book Ever.* Like most informational books for beginning readers, these books presented the material in story and pictorial form. When he started reading, Paul returned to these books on his own and also enjoyed reading *The Bears' Almanac* by S. and J. Berenstain (a description of seasonal changes in story form) and a dictionary with words arranged according to categories (more manageable for him as a five-year-old than straight alphabetical order). When he was six years old, joke and riddle books had functioned as a sort of informational resource. Paul's reading ability at 7:7 was advanced enough for him to read the more directly presented information characteristic of books beyond the primary level. It was not only Paul's reading interests that had changed but the materials available to him. His television interests were changing, too. As a seven-year-old he had graduated from young children's shows and was watching more story-type afternoon and early evening programs, which provided "fiction" in another form.

Paul read aloud to me several of his favorite pages from *The I Hate Mathematics! Book* and then hugged me because I gave him this book that he loves so much. He has returned to it as an eight- and nine-year-old, and I have repeatedly been aware of how much he learned from it as particular incidents bring out his knowledge. Another favorite book of this period was *The Guinness* (even after I corrected him, Paul still preferred "genius") *Book of World Records,* again a book that he kept returning to and the first of a number of factual compendiums. (Later he enjoyed the *Believe It or Not* books, and collections of assorted facts by Arkady Leokum such as *The Curious Book.*) Paul shared interesting information by reading selections aloud or just reporting the information. He used his dictionary not so much to look up unfamiliar words — he usually asked the meaning of these — but as another source of interesting facts, such as how many different meanings a word had.

He enjoyed the freedom of selective reading — of dipping into informational books wherever he wanted and not necessarily reading from beginning to end. This was one approach to reading that appropriately developed more as he moved into informational texts. Paul was impressed enough by the introduction to *The Reasons for Seasons* (though he was not crazy about this science book) to imitate it in his own writing. The introduction read in part:

> This is not a regular page 1 to page 128 book.
> The pages are to be used in any order you like.
> So if you want to, jump in at the middle — or
> somewhere near the end.
> However you fancy . . .
>
> The directions in this book are written in a general way.
> That is because there is no such thing
> as The Right Way to do anything.
> If you don't like this way, try that way.
> But mostly try it — and have a good time.*

---

*From L. Allison, *The Reasons for Seasons* (Boston: Little, Brown, 1975), p. 5.

Paul's introduction to his "Fun Book," written at 7:8, said:

> This is not a regular book if you want to you can skip to the middle or somewhere near the end or you can just work your way through anyway it's fun.

At 7:9 his father got him an encyclopedia, *The New Book of Knowledge* (mostly fifth to sixth grade level), which Paul used increasingly over the following two years as a source of independent reading and a resource for school projects. He was already locating information in indexes and tables of contents, which he had included in the books he wrote since more than a year earlier.

He also skimmed for information, as he demonstrated while looking at an archaeology book with me one day (7:9) and skimming the text to find what century various works in the photographs dated from. He skimmed, too, when he was reading from D. C. Beard's *The American Boys' Handy Book* (8:0); he also simply skipped passages that did not interest him. As he read this, he whistled and gurgled—evidence that, for all the noise, his reading was truly silent and not whispered (as when he started to read silently) or even subvocalized.

As an eight-year-old Paul talked about the new information he learned through reading at school and on his own. He quizzed his parents to see if we knew it, and was disappointedly surprised when we did. It was all new and exciting to him as he made his way into the larger world beyond family, school, and community by filling himself with information about it.

Most of Paul's mental energy seemed to be directed to the sheer acquisition of information—to "literal comprehension." At least that is what he talked about most; perhaps his thinking as well as his reading was silent by this time. Occasionally he spontaneously showed that he had thought further about some piece of information or added something of his own to it. At 8:6 he was reading a book on language and word origins, which included this passage:

IF THERE WERE NO WORDS
  Without words, people couldn't learn anything except by finding it out for themselves. And they could not tell others what they had learned. Nobody, for example, could tell anyone

else that fire is hot. A person could learn that only by burning
himself.*

That evening Paul commented that this would be a silly world
without language. If a man burned his hand on a stove, he
would not be able to tell other people it was hot. If he pushed
them away, they would not know why. Although he did not
repeat the generalization about language and learning, he was
vividly impressed with the point as demonstrated through a
particular situation, which he had elaborated in his own mind.

Paul made — or at least verbalized — more spontaneous in-
ferences from facts of his experience than from facts he had
read, such as his rediscovery that the earth moves from observing the flattening of a rectangle of light projected by a prism in
third grade. But during this whole period (7:7-9:11) he was
more fascinated by facts than generalizations, more interested
in concrete explanations than theories.

On a visit to the library shortly before his ninth birthday
Paul chose these books:

> *Spooky Tricks* (magic — he was performing magic tricks himself
>   and eagerly sought out further sources of tricks)
> *The Magic Man* and *Masters of Magic* (he was distressed to find
>   that these were biographies of magicians and not how-to
>   books)
> *Strings on Your Fingers* (making string figures)
> *Puttering with Paper* (science experiments)
> *Lumberjack* (describing a lumberjack's work)
> *The Bread Book: About Bread and How to Make It*
> *Danny Dunn and the Weather Machine* and *Danny Dunn and the Voice
>   from Space*

The emphasis, even in the last two fictional books, is on making, inventing, and doing things — very much in keeping with
Paul's active approach to life.

As a fourth grader Paul was required to do much more informational reading for school, especially encyclopedia reading to
get facts on foreign countries for Social Studies work. Independently he continued to read for information, becoming

---

*From S. and B. Epstein, *What's Behind the Word?* (New York: Scholastic,
1964), p. 4.

immersed in it for longer stretches and doing more rereading. He read and reread most of the Brown Paper School books— *The I Hate Mathematics! Book* (an all-time favorite), *The Book of Think* (his second favorite in this series), *Everybody's a Winner, The Reasons for Seasons, My Backyard History Book, I Am Not a Short Adult!* and *Blood and Guts.* He enjoyed collections of interesting and startling facts like *Believe It or Not, The Great Disasters,* and *The Curious Book.* He read *Star Wars,* a novel by George Lucas, at 9:7 but treated it as informational by writing numerous factual quizzes on it (to be described further in the next section).

Noninformational Reading

Paul's reading of noninformational texts (mainly fiction) did not noticeably change during the earlier part of this "diversified reading" period from the way it had been during the previous period. He read full-length books, averaging about fifth to sixth grade level, in installments over several days or weeks. He also read comics (*Richie Rich* was his favorite series) and magazines (*Mad, The Electric Company, Wow*) and reread his Tintin books. This adventure series in comic format has had the most enduring interest for Paul of any reading material. He loved hearing them read aloud before he could read, and he has continued to read and reread them through the entire time covered by this study—about five years during a period of rapid growth changes. At 8:0 he reread four Tintins in one morning, but it was only somewhat later (8:5) that he read new, full-length books in one day.

At the same time Paul was getting into *The I Hate Mathematics! Book,* he was enjoying *Soup and Me,* Robert Newton Peck's stories based on his Vermont boyhood. A selection from a transcript of his taped oral reading from it will serve to illustrate Paul's reading of fiction at this time (7:7). (Compare the earlier transcripts of *Curious George* at 6:6 and "One Inch Tall" at 6:9 in Chapter 9.) The words Paul omitted in his reading are given in brackets; readings that otherwise diverge from the text are italicized.

1.   . . . Not that we were afraid of the
2. dark, you understand. Just a gesture (*guesture*) of true (*too
   . . . true*) friendship (*friend—friendship*)

3. Then we said so long, [as] Soup ran lickety (*lick — lickety*)-
   split for his
4. house and I ran [for] home.
5.   Saturday morning found (*found — found*) me up, dressed,
   [my] break-
6. fast eaten, and my chores all (*all my chores*) done. I was just
   throwing
7. the last handful of cracked corn (*in*)to our ducks when I saw
8. Soup coming down the pasture on a dead run. His feet
9. made green footsteps (*foot — footsteps*) on the early gray dew
   (*gray dew . . . on the early gray dew*) of the short
10. meadow grass. He was waving his arms and shouting
    (*shouting — shouting*)
11. but [as] he was so out of breath from the run, (*a*) few of his
12. words were audible (*addidóobullen-doo-bul-bul-bul*). When he
    finally pulled up short in (*up in a short . . . When he finally
    pulled up short in*)
13. our barnyard, he had to plunk himself down on a bale
14. of hay to let his breath catch up (*to catch his — to let his breath
    catch up*).*

Compared to Paul's six-year-old readings, there is more
evidence here of reading in word groups (not word by word),
longer eye-voice span, and anticipating of phrases:

text: . . . and my chores all done.
Paul: . . . and all my chores done.
text: . . . to let his breath catch up.
Paul: . . . to catch his — to let his breath catch up.

Paul anticipated "to catch his breath" from seeing ahead to
"catch" and "breath." The two non-words ("guesture" and "addi-
doobullen") for unfamiliar ones ("gesture" and "audible") are
the only errors evidencing a sounding-out strategy. On the second one he took a moment to make fun of himself and the
word: "addidoobullen-doo-bul-bul-bul." Most errors that
would affect comprehension and two that would not — "gray
dew" for "early gray dew" and "to catch his (breath)" for "to let
his breath catch up" — were self-corrected. Self-corrections were
characteristic of Paul's reading, and so was the repetition of

*From R. N. Peck, *Soup and Me* (New York: Knopf, 1975), p. 42. (Line arrangements as in the original.)

words. In this passage the repetitions where no error had been made occurred for reasons I can only guess at. Two of these may have been by way of rechecking and confirming text that was incongruent with his expectations: "found" (line 5) is unusual following "Saturday morning"; and Paul may have anticipated a direct quotation after "shouting" (line 10). The other three repetitions I have no explanation for. They occur in compound words ("friendship," "lickety-split," and "footsteps"), although Paul did not hesitate over the other three compound words in the passage ("understand," "breakfast," and "barnyard").

Paul's oral reading speed of about 125 words per minute here on relatively unfamiliar material (I think he had heard or read these stories once before this reading) was an increase from 110 words per minute on the unfamiliar "One Inch Tall" ten months earlier. His silent reading speed, which I determined for the first time on *Soup and Me,* was 185 words per minute, nearing an average adult rate. He expressed his own sense of increased silent reading speed when he estimated (at 8:0) that he could reread four Tintin books in less than an hour and a quarter and thought the one he had just finished had taken him fifteen minutes. I think he overestimated his speed—which would have been roughly 800 words per minute—but not his *sense* of speed. This sort of increase enabled him, five months later, to start reading entire books in one day.

The day after Christmas (8:5), Paul picked up a new fiction book and read the first ten chapters (70 pages) when he got up in the morning and the rest (53 pages) in the afternoon. His total reading time was two hours, and I estimated that his silent reading speed was nearly the same as on *Soup and Me,* about 183 words per minute. The book was *Blood in the Snow* by Marlene Shyer, recommended for grades 5 and up. Two months later (8:7) when Paul spent a school vacation day with his father, in his office and on a professional trip with him, Paul read both Roald Dahl's *Charlie and the Chocolate Factory* (162 pages—a book his third grade teacher had read aloud earlier in the year) and *Charlie and the Great Glass Elevator* (163 pages). Reading two full books in one day was unusual; generally Paul did not have such stretches of quiet time when he needed to entertain himself. Almost a year and a half later, when he picked up these books to reread them, he recalled the day he had read both of them together—a memorable event for him, too.

Obviously Paul was reading this material very fluently and was able to concentrate on reading for extended periods. Usually he did not comment a lot on fiction while he was reading, nor afterwards—often just some expression of enjoyment (like "That was really a good book") plus recounting an incident that stood out for him. I did not probe his comprehension, which seemed rather a private matter in his independent reading of fiction. He did not need to share stories as he needed to share informational material, from which he delighted in recounting interesting and amazing facts. Perhaps he sensed that informational material was more impersonal and public; perhaps talking about it as well as reading it satisfied a need to master, through knowledge, as much of the larger, external world as he could as he grew out of childhood. Stories (and poems) were more for personal enjoyment.

Although Paul could and did sometimes read informational material for long stretches of time, duration did not seem as important as for reading fiction. The plot of a novel is a large unit, whereas interesting and useful facts, which tended to be the focus of Paul's informational reading rather than encompassing theories and broad perspectives, can be gathered in shorter installments.

The first adult-level novel he read was *Star Wars* (eleventh to twelfth grade reading level) at 9:8. The *Star Wars* craze had hit: most of his friends had seen the movie and talked about it, and magazine articles about its production and stars were appearing. Paul thus had some background for reading the book even though he had not seen the film. As with other fiction, Paul enjoyed long periods of immersion in the story, but he also treated it as an object of study and a source of various projects like numerous *Star Wars* quizzes and a tape recording of excerpts from the book. He treated it more like informational material, which he clearly knew it was not. Some of his quiz questions were based on information about the movie production, and some were factual questions about the novel. He wrote a quiz on each main character or group of characters. This "Luke Skywalker Quiz" is typical:

1. Who plays Luke?
2. What is his uncle's first name?
3. Who killed his father?
4. Who killed his aunt and uncle?
5. How old is he in the movie?
6. Who are his servants?
7. How did he get them?
8. Who did he get them from?
9. Did he ever hit a TIE fighter?
10. What kind of farm does his uncle own?
11. Was it his idea to get in the trash compactor?
12. Luke's light saber was his . . .
13. How old is he in real life?
14. He grew up in . . . 8, 6, 10, 2, 3 or 5 cities?
15. What is his home planet?

An excerpt from Paul's oral reading shows that unfamiliar vocabulary is a main source of errors. He did not struggle with these words but rapidly produced a phonetic approximation to the words and moved ahead. For more than two years — since he had begun to read fluently — Paul had seemed to immediately size up difficult words as familiar or unfamiliar and did not bother working over the ones he would not understand anyway. He could pronounce long and unfamiliar words correctly, as he demonstrated several times on lists of isolated words, but in reading continuous text for himself he made a judgment about whether it was worth the effort. In this *Star Wars* passage Paul self-corrected his one clearly semantically unacceptable error, amending "inquired to his" to "inquired of his":

> Threepio turned his smooth, humanlike head to one side. Metallic ears listened intently. The imitation of a human pose was hardly necessary — Threepio's auditory sensors (*sensitors*) were fully omnidirectional — but the slim robot had been programmed to blend perfectly among human company. This program[ming] extended even to (*to even*) mimicry of human gestures.

"Did you hear that?" he inquired rhetorically of his (*rehorléti-cally to his . . . of his*) patient companion, referring to the throb-bing sound. "They['ve] shut down the main reactor and the drive." His voice was [as] full of disbelief and concern as that of any human. One metallic palm rubbed dolefully at a patch of dull gray on his side, where a broken hull brace had fallen and scored the bronze finish. Threepio was a fastidious (*fástidous*) machine, and such things troubled him.*

Paul's gain in oral reading fluency since reading *Soup and Me* a little over two years earlier is not evident in a words per minute count: about 140 words per minute on *Star Wars* com-pared to about 125 on *Soup and Me.* But the majority of words in the earlier book were monosyllabic, while the majority in *Star Wars* were polysyllabic. In terms of syllables per minute, his reading was 70 percent faster. *Star Wars* used more complex and inverted sentence structures than *Soup and Me,* and Paul's greater familiarity with these structures is evident from the in-tonations on his recording.

One thing that Paul learned from reading was "book lan-guage" or "dialect"—the vocabulary and syntactic forms that tend to occur in written language but not in informal speech. During all those years he was read aloud to he was becoming accustomed to "book language." As the materials he read became more and more advanced, their language became more and more distinct from everyday speech. In conversation with his parents at least, Paul's speech even showed signs of "book dialect": "When we got back from the playground there was something very troubling" (7:3); "I'm going to pack my stuff for Plum Island in this manner" (9:1).

Perhaps a month after his first reading of *Star Wars,* Paul reread it and was amazed at how much he had missed the first time. Rereading books was characteristic of Paul during the last few months covered by this chapter—the months before his tenth birthday. Larrick has observed of avid third and fourth grade readers that "often they go back to a favorite book and re-read it or its sequel four or five times" (1975, p. 77). Three times was Paul's record. At six years old he had reread books in

---

*From G. Lucas, *Star Wars* (New York: Ballantine Books, 1976), pp. 4-5.

order to gain fluency in reading as well as to return to favorite stories. At nine years old both his reading development and his reading materials had changed enough to change also the nature of his rereadings. If he was "practicing" now, it was his comprehension rather than his decoding skills — rereading to understand or remember more about a topic or a story. Most of the material was rich enough to offer something new upon rereading as well as the renewal of an old friendship.

This chapter ends with Paul as a reader somewhere in the midst of "diversified reading." His changes are less obvious now; the time that he spends in each successive period of his reading development increases as his strategies and purposes and materials become more complex and comprehensive — as there is more to elaborate and grow on. Any description of a mature reader will point up directions in which Paul will later grow as a reader, but exactly how and when he will get there — those specifics that are the lifeblood of a case study — I will not even speculate on. Instead of ending this chapter with a glance toward the future, I end it with a close look at the present: Paul as a reader just before his tenth birthday.

He has been picking up free literature (mostly advertising) in every store and public place he sees it. He actually reads it — as he devours almost anything in print — and has put a large box of the stuff in the bathroom for reading material. As bedtime reading he has been going through his carton of old Richie Rich comics. He is also rereading Roald Dahl's *Danny, the Champion of the World,* which he had read months ago; he recounted the incident of feeding the drugged raisins to the pheasants and said he did not remember how the book ended. On the Fourth of July he stayed up until one in the morning to read all 188 pages of *The Mad Scientists' Club,* which I had picked up for him at a used book sale that evening. His increased fiction reading may be balancing out his decreased television watching.

On a trip to our summer cottage one weekend when he packed clothes but no books, he eagerly read *The Tooth Trip,* a lively book on preventive dental care that I had bought for myself, and recounted quite a few interesting and complicated bits of information. The next weekend his suitcase was packed with practically no clothes and seven books: *Charlie and the Chocolate Factory* (to reread), *The Magic Book,* and five of his Brown Paper School books (*The Book of Think, I Am Not a Short Adult, My Backyard History Book, Everybody's a Winner,* and *The I Hate Mathematics! Book*). He did not begin to read them all on that trip.

12 Summary of Paul's Reading Development

Before he could decode words, Paul was rehearsing reading by turning the pages in a book while "reading" the familiar story from the pictures (two and a half years old). This looked and sounded like reading, and involved most of the basic spatial orientations and principles of reading except identification of printed words. By five years old he began identifying words, at first using nonverbal context clues (such as the location and appearance of highway signs, and perhaps word configuration, to read "exit") and then matching spoken to printed words by using initial and final letter-sound relationships (as when he identified "circus" on his bookstore list by its ending in *s*). This kind of matching requires a clear expectation of what the word might be, which at this stage can only come from context clues or familiarity with what the text says, as with a story. He must have understood that there was only one correct spoken equivalent for a printed word. As a five-year-old beginning reader he moved into decoding, using sound-letter relationships more fully to figure out words in short texts. When he started to read longer texts, he made more use of verbal context clues.

Just before he turned six, Paul evidently had mastered enough of the mechanics of decoding to focus on increasing his speed and on reading in phrase and sentence units, letting phonic approximations stand for some hard words to be corrected if subsequent context enabled. After about a year and a half of gaining fluency on noninformational texts, Paul extended his mastery of the "objective," basically adult world by branching out into informational reading. He still read fiction and other noninformational material, but diversified his approach to different kinds of texts.

What may appear on the surface and through standardized test results as *quantitative* changes — reading more words, longer books, more kinds of material, more words per minute — arise from *qualitative* changes in reading strategies and purposes, not merely from more of the same skills (like acquiring more sight words). Development — and Paul's development in particular — is not evenly paced. There is more rapid movement through the earlier strategies and concepts because these are more limited and incomplete in relation to the demands of the task. Especially at the beginning, quite drastic change seems essential for progress. It may not matter so much where a child begins in reading (phonics, sight words, language experience) as that he begins *somewhere* that works for him and soon moves somewhere *else*. Later strategies, being more inclusive and complex, allow room for more extended development. Chall's first two reading stages take one or two years each, while her next two stages span about three years each. The development of mature reading skills seems to involve a long period of learning and growth through reading phases of increasing duration.

Paul's reading, like his writing, can be viewed as a matter of cognitive development or as an aspect of personal development. Change has been the focus of my account of Paul's reading as cognitive growth; continuity is the emphasis when personal characteristics such as interests and style of response are held in view. Many of the books Paul enjoyed having read aloud to him were books he returned to when he was able to read. His reading interests as a seven-year-old included the kinds of material he read through his ninth year — science fiction, adventure stories, humorous stories, and informational books with an emphasis on remarkable facts and scientific kinds of information. He was an active learner, experimenting and finding things out for himself; he preferred inventing, con-structing, and elaborating to following directions precisely; he had strong interests and even as a very beginning reader worked at home for extended, concentrated stretches of time. He did not use his capacities as fully in school, perhaps because of the routine nature and unchallenging level of some of the assignments, and perhaps also because his self-directedness did not yield to teacher direction.

13 Educational Implications for Reading

Because of the nature and conditions of classroom instruction, children who must learn to read in school may have a harder task in some ways than children who learn at home. Except for Torrey's remarkable child, children who learned at home received considerable parental attention — if not instruction, then responses to their questions about reading. Research by the Educational Testing Service (McDonald, 1976) indicated that the critical variable for teacher effectiveness in second grade reading was direct individual instruction: a "tutorial model" with teachers using a variety of materials and providing prompt instruction and correction to individuals and small groups rather than whole-class teaching with students doing unmonitored seatwork and waiting for teacher attention. Tutorial-type teaching is more apt to occur at home than in a classroom of twenty to thirty children.

Considering the sheer *amount* of reading Paul had done over these five years, I would expect him to be "ahead." From observing him and other fluent readers who read frequently, and from teaching older children with reading difficulties who read as little as possible, I see practice being as crucial for reading success as for playing basketball or piano or any other skill. Clay (1972) has estimated from her classroom observations that children making superior progress had read 20,000 words in their first year of instruction at school, average readers between 10,000 and 15,000, and slow readers probably less than 5,000. This does not include the amount of reading done at home, which would increase the difference between the fluent and slower readers. It is easy to see how this gap continues to widen over the years. Amount of reading may be a key to the continued advantage both Durkin and Clark observed in their early readers through school.

The sacredness of "reading time" in bed before he went to sleep contributed to the amount of reading Paul did. I suppose this began to be established before he could read, during the years his parents regularly read to him at bedtime. He spent roughly fifteen to thirty minutes a night reading, in addition to the varying amounts he read during the day. In school settings, a regular silent reading period may serve this purpose.

One important form of practice for Paul was rereading books. If this was important to a successful reader, consider how important it might be to some children having difficulty. Perhaps it gave Paul, as a beginning reader, clearer feedback on his own progress; he could tell he was reading the same book more fluently than before. I have seen remedial students measure their progress this way. If a child's growth in reading is measured in terms of his pace in moving through a series of increasingly difficult books, it is hard to see the value of rereading. The books that Paul reread were favorites, books whose world he really wanted to reenter, so personal selection of material was important for this kind of practice.

Paul's reading materials certainly did not have a controlled vocabulary in the sense of a limited number of words repeated from book to book with gradual additions. However, he exercised another kind of control through his choice of short texts (labels, for example) as beginning reading materials. Since his basic beginning reading strategy involved using letter-sound relationships (through writing he had a lot of practice with "phonics") plus context rather than sight word recognition, the lack of vocabulary repetition was not a problem. In fact it may have fostered the development of multiple strategies, which then enabled Paul to see and self-correct errors. Because he generally attended to letter-sound relationships, meaning, and syntax, I did not feel obliged to point out or correct every error. My silence sometimes enabled me to observe delayed self-corrections that could not have occurred had I addressed errors as soon as they were made. Perhaps it also encouraged him to assume responsibility for correcting his own reading.

Compared to the choice of materials Paul would have had as a beginning reader in most classrooms, his was wide. Nonetheless, it was limited and directed by the choices of his adult book-providers—entirely as a pre-reader and beginning reader, but less as he grew older and had access to libraries, book clubs, and so forth. He was of course free to reject books, which he sometimes did (especially fairy tales); and as his main book supplier, I tried to pick books that were in line with his interests. Many of his best-loved books throughout the years of this study were books that had been chosen for him. When he went to bookstores and libraries with his parents, he tended to look for one title or type of book rather than browsing through the shelves as an adult might. I was clearly more familiar with the arrangement of bookstores and libraries and with the kinds of books available. I think I kept in mind a more comprehensive view of Paul's reading interests than he did, even as a nine-year-old. Most of the books Paul first read when he turned to informational reading were parent-supplied: *The I Hate Mathematics! Book,* his dictionary, and his encyclopedia. From age seven on, his reading was increasingly influenced by his peers: other children in second grade were reading *The Guinness Book of World Records;* a friend in third grade had *The Book of Think* and some Moomin books, which Paul then wanted to read; and in the fourth grade the *Star Wars* craze was near universal, though only a few of his friends had actually read the book and not just seen the movie. For even as self-directed a reader as Paul, considerable adult input in selecting materials was important since he did not have the experience to know what was available to choose from. I feel sure that having at hand material that appealed to him further motivated his reading, especially as he grew older and, like an adult, read independently mainly because of interest in the content.

Case studies of other beginning readers who more or less

selected their own materials would help us to see how important personal reading interests may be from the start. Are interests a more crucial factor in motivating children who learn to
read on their own than those who learn in school, where other
kinds of motivations are operating? Clark's research on young
fluent readers led her to observe that "the early reading of boys
was more likely to be associated with their other interests, while
the girls aimed at extending their reading of stories" (1976, p.
11). This parallels Graves's observation (1975) of sex differences in the writing interests of young children.

Paul gained much early reading practice on non-book
materials like cereal boxes, labels, and signs. Clark's study suggests that this, too, may reflect a sex difference: "While a
number of the children were first attracted to reading through
stories, a number began with signs, advertisements, or letter
games. Although these early reading experiences for some of
the children were in books from which they had enjoyed stories,
for some of the children the print in their immediate environment played an important role. This was particularly true of
boys who showed interest in signposts, car names, captions on
television and names on products in supermarkets" (Clark,
1976, p. 51).

Through almost all of his first year of reading, Paul read
aloud. Most of Clark's fluent readers "appeared to read silently
either from the beginning or from an early stage which made it
difficult for parents to pin-point exactly when they began to
read" (1976, p. 102). It seems that beginning readers differ
markedly in their starting points — the materials, reading interests, and strategies that bring them into reading. A collection of case studies — such as those already gathered by the
Prospect School in North Bennington, Vermont (unpublished)
and those being gathered for the Collaborative Research Project of the Early Education Research Group (Educational
Testing Service) — reveal a great range of differences among
children as readers and writers.

In observing one child we are also observing much that is
common to other children. What we cannot know, until we
observe others, is how much of what we see is common and
how much idiosyncratic. We look for the commonalities, and

perhaps overlook the value of the differences. If all children learned in exactly the same way, all teachers would have to teach in exactly the same way. That children can learn in a variety of ways may be nature's design for ensuring that they will learn in the face of the differences they encounter in their environments.

Part Three

Writing and Reading

14 Writing and Reading Converge: Paul, Ten Years Old

Changes in Paul's writing and reading did not—as I anticipated—simply continue to appear more gradually as he grew older. The logic of growth took my logic by surprise: his eleventh year revealed new developments as well as established activities taking new directions. Paul's reading and writing came together as never before through writings that resembled or imitated in style and content some of his favorite reading material—science fiction stories and humor magazines. Extensive revisions became evident in his writing. His interest in newspapers, which had shown itself so early and developed so persistently, took new turns not only through magazine production but also because Paul now involved some of his friends in this and others of his writing projects and had a larger audience for his writings at school. As peers assumed more importance in his life, Paul engaged them in a variety of magazine writing projects and in writing the script for and producing a science fiction movie. His intensified reading of science fiction was also shared with one or two close friends who discussed and exchanged books.

The confluence of writing and reading, the socialization of these activities, and the process of revision are the themes of this chapter.

Paul's writing activities were mainly initiated by himself—the *Battlestar Galactica* sequel he wrote and the two issues of the *Twinfield Gossip,* followed by two issues of *Strange* magazine and a couple of other single-issue productions. At his father's suggestion that he make a movie (rather than watch so much television), he started on a movie script, *The Gem of Chrondo.* Paul's fifth grade teacher required little sustained writing but rather workbooks, worksheets, and reading conferences. Paul's spontaneous writings became incorporated into his school setting, however, when he sold *Strange* magazine in the lunch line, when the librarian put a copy in the school library, and when he and his coeditor, Rowan, taught a mini-course in magazine production to other fifth graders. During the latter part of the year a weekly period was established for mini-courses taught by parents, teachers, and students. Paul and Rowan had the idea to teach a magazine production course, got their teacher's approval, and with their "students" produced *Something for All.*

Paul's teacher ran an individualized reading program and, knowing his interest, tried to supply him with science fiction. Although Paul read H. G. Wells's *The Time Machine and Other Stories* (which he found difficult) at school, most of the selections available in his classroom were children's stories such as the Marvin Mooney series. Paul enjoyed these but also C. S. Lewis's Narnia series, which he borrowed from a friend. When making his own selections at a bookstore, Paul chose mostly adult anthologies of short science fiction stories, such as *The Science Fiction Hall of Fame* and *Science Fiction of the 40's* (at 10:10). He had started his science fiction reading with novels, from *The Day of the Ness,* when he was seven, through *Star Wars* and several other more or less adult novels as a nine- and ten-year-old.

In sum, Paul's writing and reading as a ten-year-old were more self- and peer-directed than school- and parent-directed. Science fiction themes and humor predominated; his writing style was strongly influenced by adult models. At 10:4 he wrote "The Death of Starbuck," a *Battlestar Galactica* sequel. He had read the first *Battlestar Galactica* novel, started on the second, and watched some of the series on television. He had also read several other current science fiction works such as *Close*

Encounters, Splinter of the Mind's Eye, and *Star Trek.* Here is chapter 2 from "The Death of Starbuck," as Paul typed it:

Scene: The GALACTICAS' sensors pick up a cylon BaseStar under very mild attack by three unknown craft.

"My god" said Adama. "What is it sir?" a puzzled Tigh asked. "Those ships are colonial fighters" the dazed Adama replied. No one needed to ask to know whose ships they were. For a while it was thought that Athena was out there too, but she was found . . pouting in a corner. Adama tried to comfort her, but to no avail.

Later, all the pilots came back, unhurt. When they announced the amazing fact that they had defeated the base star, a party was thrown in their honor.

Apollos' father asked why thier scanners hadn't picked it up, he replied, "They found a leak in our camoflage screen and analyzed it and made an exact duplicate." Then his father asked "Then how did you find it?" "It was simple," replied Apollo. "They made the duplicate SO perfect, that they also reproduced the leak." "But why did you go in the first place"? a grateful Athena asked, obviously focusing on Starbuck. "Because we wanted to prove that we DID see something out there" said Boomer, without thinking. he felt an elbow in his gut. But it was too late. There was no way he could take it back . . .

For comparison, here is an excerpt from *Battlestar Galactica:*

The elevator door opened, and the raucous noise of the bridge drowned out the remainder of Starbuck's question. Angry, he stormed into the room. Nobody noticed him. The voice of one of the bridge officers rose over the clamor.

"Fighter ships coming in on both decks, sir."

Tigh moved toward the officer and said:

"Give me a full report. What's the count?"

Tigh? Starbuck thought. What's he doing giving the orders? Where's Adama? There can't be anything wrong with Adama! He felt disoriented, thrust into some alternate world where Adama no longer existed and the terrible cowardice of removing the *Galactica* from her proper place had somehow been transformed into heroism.

"Sixty-seven fighters in all, sir, twenty-five of our own."

"How many battlestars?"

The officer paused before revealing the information.

"None."

"What?!"

"We're the only surviving battlestar."

"My God." Tigh looked shocked. When he spoke again, it was in a choked voice. "Make the pilots from the other ships as welcome as you can."*

When I asked Paul if he was trying to write "The Death of Starbuck" like the *Battlestar Galactica* novels, he asked, "You mean the style?" Yes, he had tried to imitate that style. Months after he had read *Battlestar Galactica* and written his story, I mentioned to Paul that I had done a readability measure on the two works, and he volunteered a guess that *Battlestar* was probably seventh to eighth grade level and his own writing probably fifth to sixth or maybe seventh grade level. He seemed more uncertain about the level of his own writing, except in estimating it as less difficult than the published work. According to the Dale-Chall formula, both were seventh to eighth grade reading level; but there were differences in range of difficulty. I chose passages of dialogue, description, and mixed types from each work; the four passages from *Battlestar* ranged from fourth to ninth or tenth grade reading levels, while those from "The Death of Starbuck" were all either at seventh to eighth grade level or just a hair below. In *Battlestar,* as in most fiction, the dialogue passage scored lowest (fourth grade level) and the descriptive passage highest (at the top of the ninth to tenth grade level score range). Changes of form — from dialogue to narrative and description — had very little effect on Paul's sentence length and vocabulary, the features directly measured by a readability formula. This was one aspect of adult style he had not imitated.

In writing "The Death of Starbuck," Paul was bringing to bear much that he had learned through reading many books; he was not imitating just *Battlestar Galactica.* Constructions such as "the dazed Adama replied" and "a grateful Athena asked" are definitely bookish but are not characteristic of *Battlestar*'s style.

Most of Paul's knowledge of punctuation came from reading,

---

*From G. A. Larson and R. Thurston, *Battlestar Galactica* (New York: Berkeley, 1978), pp. 63-64.

such as his use of the colon ("Scene: The GALACTICAS' sensors") and ellipses ("but she was found . . . pouting in a corner"). Paul had not accepted the convention of three ellipsis points, but varied the number apparently according to the length of pause, degree of suspense, or extent of implication intended, as evident in other chapters of "The Death of Starbuck": "Now here's what we'll do................" and "But we thought you were.......dead!" Although he had been given no instruction on the semicolon, he wrote in the last chapter: "The news spread so quickly that before they could stop the fleet to declare a holiday, everyone was out looking for Starbuck; but no one could find him." When I asked Paul about the semicolon, he said he had seen it in reading and started using it when a comma or a period would not fit. He was uncomfortable about trying to articulate a rule, saying initially that he "guessed" where to use the semicolon although he had used it conventionally here and in other writings during this year. His formal instruction on the comma had not included uses such as he demonstrated in this sentence from "Starbuck": "Later, all the pilots came back, unhurt." "That I definitely got from reading," Paul said. He seems to have learned punctuation much as he learned spelling, vocabulary, and syntax — from observation and practice through which he drew his own operational rules. So do other youngsters. A science fiction story by an eighth grade boy that I read recently confirms a similar learning of sentence structures and punctuation from reading.

Paul's misplaced apostrophes (GALACTICAS', Apollos'), when viewed in the light of other possessive apostrophes in the rest of the story, do not look like simple errors in placement, for he also wrote "Boomer's" and "Starbuck's." Only when words ended in a vowel did he put the apostrophe after the *s*: Adamas', Galacticas', Apollos', Cassiopeas', and Serinas'. When I asked him about this, he said he was trying to use a rule that he had been taught but did not understand.

One thing Paul had not picked up from reading was conventional paragraphing for dialogue. His paragraphing, as in the chapter quoted from "Starbuck," was strictly based on shifts in topic or time — an analysis he confirmed. He did not see or choose to adopt some conventions of written language or some uses of those conventions. The dashes liberally used in *Battlestar Galactica* were never incorporated into his writing. Thus even "imitation" can be a form of selective learning, controlled by the learner and by the knowledge and purposes he comes to his models with.

Paul had started writing "The Death of Starbuck" by hand but then typed over his beginning and continued the story on the typewriter. Since he did not cross out or write changes on the handwritten draft, I was not immediately aware of his revisions. Talking with Paul later about revisions, I learned that he usually did write a first draft and then make changes as he typed the final copy: "Whenever I rewrite something, I usually change it. I hardly ever leave it the same." He said he did not copy writing over just for the sake of neatness. "If something doesn't sound good or look good, I'll change it."

He had made some changes in "A Magic Carpet or Two" when he was eight, he told me. Sometimes he would write a section at school, then the next day reread it and see it differently; but the changes involved erasing and changing only a few words. He said he sometimes considered alternatives mentally before writing, but at other times wrote fast so he would not forget an idea. ("I did that once and I didn't like it.") Even as a five-year-old he had revised mentally as he considered signing his letter to Jeanne Chall "from Paul" or "Paul wrote that above," and ended up writing at the top of the letter PAUL ROT THES. As a six-year-old he had revised his oral reading of Shel Silverstein's poem "Lazy Jane" several times until it sounded the way he wanted it. His block constructions and later his Lego block designs were repeatedly revised. Graves has observed that "children revise in other media forms such as block building, drawing and painting before they revise in writing. Children who demonstrate an overall learning stance toward revision in one area are more likely to demonstrate it in another such as writing" (Graves, 1979a, p. 318).

Paul was a reviser, but extensive revision and editing of his writings seems a ten-year-old development. Had he revised the beginning of "The Death of Starbuck" on his original draft rather than typing a second version, it would have looked like the writer's worksheet shown in figure 9. "That's quite a few

Scene: Starbuck, Boomer and Apollo are on patrol.

"Hey Boom-Boom" said Starbuck. "*S*ee anything?"

"Negative" "How about cutting in the thrusters and see

what/s out there" replied Boomer. "Hold it you guys"

a voice cut in. It was Apollo, commander Adama's son.

"Why does he always have to ~~butt in~~ *spoil our fun*?" (Starbuck) remarked.

~~"Look, Starbuck, we have to follow orders" "But....."~~

~~He turned his head as if to see a cylon warship monitoring~~

~~his thoughts. "I'm with you" he turned his head again.~~

~~"Let's go" "I always new you...."~~ ~~Boomer's sentence was~~ *Apollo was about to say something*

when a whole sqadron of ~~interrupted by ten~~ *c*ylon warships streak~~ing~~ *ed* overhead.

"They went right ~~past~~ *by* us!" shrieked starbuck. ~~"I know"~~

(said Apollo). "You forget ~~starbuck~~,"were still enveloped

in the energy field surrounding the fleet." "Oh, yeah"

said *S*tarbuck, embar/assed. "I kinda forgot" "Hey you guys"

a voice cut in, "Sorry to interrupt your discussion, but

how about reporting back to the Galactica?"

Figure 9. *Revision of "The Death of Starbuck" (10:4) as it might have looked had Paul revised on his original draft.*

changes!" Paul exclaimed when I showed him his revisions in this form. The changes are on several levels. A whole chunk of dialogue that did not advance the action is cut from the middle of this passage. Looking back on it, Paul commented that he cut it "probably because it didn't have much to do with the story." Such cuts require sufficient vision of the purpose and direction of the piece of writing to eliminate elements not in keeping with that overall design. Smaller-scale revisions include three changes in wording, one substantial insertion, two changes in word order, and two short deletions. Paul also edited for mechanics; punctuation, spelling, capitalization, and paragraphing changes were made.

Revisions made in the process of typing a final copy also occurred later this year in *Strange* magazine. The "STRANGE Publishing Office" sign on Paul's bedroom door declared his self-consciousness as a writer. The door was locked so I did not observe the editor at work nor realize until most of the original drafts had been destroyed that he was revising. Paul did find one original page for me, the second page of his first edition (10:6). The changes — initiated by the need to alter the initial narrow column arrangement to accommodate a wide picture — were so drastic that the two versions must be read side by side:

(original draft)
AND NOW....
What do you think this
STRANGE thing is?
    [picture]
Well, if you guessed
that it was a MORAY EEL,
you're right! This cute
little sucker only lives
in warm water. What am
I saying little for?
This guy can grow up
to 10 feet (foots) long!
Don't get too close now,
he's been known to bite!
    [picture]
    [column 2]
Did ya see the lil'
critter on the other
page? Well that's
the shoebill stork.
(Cute, ain't he?)
His beak is *very*
heavy. He also likes
to sleep all day and
look for food at night.

(revision)
STRANGE PICTURES
Here are two STRANGE
pictures. This one
is a MORAY EEL,
    [picture]
And this one is the
SHOEBILL STORK.
    [picture]
    [column 2]
The MORAY EEL only lives
in warm water. He can
grow up to ten feet (22
snerods) long! Then there
is the SHOEBILL STORK,
Whose beak is very heavy.
(5 blurks!) He sleeps all
day and looks for food at
night.

Six months later, when I found out about this revision and asked Paul why he made it, he could not tell me. Perhaps it reflects his concern with the tone of the magazine; he had commented that "it started out more strange and became more humorous." In this revision early in his writing of the magazine, Paul curbed a humorous style (which eventually won out) in order to focus on the strange aspects of his subject.

Reading influenced his magazine writing in several ways. The information he selected for STRANGE facts and for STRANGE places, as well as the news reports and advertisements that he parodied, came largely from his reading. (Paul had understood the word "satire" since he was eight years old through his reading of *Mad* magazine.) The style of *Strange* was certainly influenced by the humor magazines Paul read, but it was not an imitation, as the style of "The Death of Starbuck" was. His use of magazine layout and writing conventions went far beyond any instruction he received: the index page, the "(cont. on next page)" notation, and the use of colons and parentheses. Reading was no less an influence on his early newspapers with their weather forecasts, advertisements, and funnies; but what Paul noticed and selected from his reading and how he adapted it in his writing changed, as did of course his reading materials themselves. How his writing, in turn, may have influenced his reading, at least in terms of what he attended to, would be interesting to explore. I know of only one instance where his writing seems to have influenced his book selection: he bought two science fiction quiz books this year after writing his own science fiction quizzes.

Paul's magazine writing, viewed as a continuation of his newspaper writing, had a new context: he was addressing his writing to an audience of his peers and working on it with a friend. Thus the increased importance of peers in his life as a ten-year-old did not diminish his writing but socialized it. According to Paul's account, he and his friend Rowan first decided that they wanted to do *some* kind of magazine. Paul chose "Strange" from several ideas, wrote up a few pages, and called Rowan to get his agreement on the decision.

Strange magazine was heavily illustrated with a few original drawings and many pictures cut out from other magazines but used for original purposes. Paul kept a collection of "strange" pictures in a cardboard box, which he used to illustrate articles he had written and to stimulate his writing. "If I'm stuck for an idea, I look through my collection of strange pictures." Rowan, according to Paul, "writes and then he tries to find pictures. One article he got an idea from a picture."

As its cover announced, this was a magazine with "STRANGE articles, STRANGE pictures, and most of all . . . STRANGE WRITERS." The following account of how its writers get their ideas, from the first issue, makes clear the deliberate creation of a wacky image of its editors:

> *OUR SECRET REVEALED AT LAST!!!*
> No, not the secret of how we stay looking so young, but the secret of how we get all of our ideas! well, to tell the truth, we saw this exercising machine (the kind that have the little belt that you slip around your waist, and you flick a switch, and it shakes the life out of you.) in a store window, and decided that there was absolutely no use for it, so naturally we bought it. We took it to the STRANGE office, where we looked it over. Suddenly we had an idea. we put it on a sturdy cement base, then attached a neck brace to it. Then we slipped our head into the belt, put our neck in the brace, and turned on the machine. imeddiately our head started shaking, and ideas were falling out all over the place. That's how we get our ideas. (10:7)

The beginnings of this humorous style and of creating a humorous characterization of himself through writing were evident a year and a half earlier in his PISTOL PAUL GONE GUNWACKY article: "Pistol Paul just baught a new pistol and is using up ammo like a lawn mower uses up gasoline. Scientists say that he must have a terrible earwax problem because anyone else in his position would be deaf by now."

As Paul was creating a character for himself, he was creating a voice for that character. Although *Strange* was composed of short pieces, it was sustained writing in terms of theme and voice. By contrast, Paul's early writings sound stiff, impersonal, and formulaic: "Once upon a time there was a bear and that bear went away and he never came back again" (5:1); "If you open cans I will give you a can opener" (5:2); "Paul is going to run around and jump and exercise" (5:8); "Sometimes I hate

school. I hate getting my work wrong. I hate getting in trouble,
I hate losing marble games" (6:11); "Once upon a time there
was a little rabbit who had no home, so he looked for one. In
the distance he could see a light. He went toward it . . . " (7:6).
Much of his early writing was also modeled after the voiceless
forms of signs, labels, instructions, newspapers, and the
writings of his first grade classmates. Only as Paul became self-
conscious as a writer and aware of an audience, at eight years
old, did his writing acquire a distinctive voice. The voice we
hear at times in "A Magic Carpet or Two," as Paul distin-
guishes between himself as narrator and character ("I suppose
you want to know how you steer a magic carpet") is his own.
The humorous voice of "Pistol Paul" and *Strange* magazine
seems influenced by his devoted reading of *Mad* magazine since
he was seven years old. As we have seen, Paul could also write
in the style of current science fiction. He could try on different
styles, role playing through writing.

He had also developed a "school" style, as in this fifth grade
piece in response to an assignment to write a comparison using
two things of his choice. His own voice breaks through in the
first paragraph:

> Comparing 2 works of science fiction
> I am writing a comparison of 2 science fiction works, and
> hoping I can finish before 9:30. The works that I am comparing
> are STAR WARS and BATTLESTAR GALACTICA.
> STAR WARS is a film that is a little more than science fic-
> tion. It has science fiction, fantasy, and a little bit of magic.
> BATTLESTAR GALACTICA has a different theme, but it
> is the same in the way that people like it. It does not, I think,
> have as much fantasy.
> To sum it up, I think that I can say safely most everyone ap-
> preciates good science fiction; and that they like the types of
> characters found in these works. The young, courageous type,
> (Luke Sky Walker, Apollo) The reckless, shoot-em-up type,
> (Han Solo, Starbuck) and the wise old man (Ben Kenobi,
> Adama.)

Through writing Paul not only expresses but explores and
becomes a many-sided, self-conscious person.

"Behavior can be understood and appraised only in terms of what has gone before and what is coming. The present is but a moment in a dynamism that stems from the past and harkens to the future" (Di Leo, 1977, p. 131). We never can begin at the beginning or arrive at the end. When I began keeping records for this study, I was not aware as I am now of the precursors of writing and reading, so I missed some beginnings such as scribbling. I am sure I will look back and see that I missed the meaning of some behaviors that only later became apparent. There is no particular reason to stop at Paul's eleventh birthday, but there are other studies to be made and one must move on.

Relationships between Writing and Reading in Paul's Development

15

Paul at 6:9 said he had a question that he had thought up, like the chicken and the egg riddle: which came first — reading or writing? He decided that writing came first because you had to have letters — or even a picture — before you could read it. The relationship between his own reading and writing is not so easy to describe because it is rather chicken and eggy; it is not simple and direct, and it is multileveled. The chicken and egg question is a problem when viewed in the context of our linear thinking with its one-directional categories of "before" and "after," "cause" and "effect," which may not describe natural processes very accurately. In Paul's case neither learning to read nor learning to write clearly came first. Although invented spelling developed rapidly at the start, writing and reading developed together, with the lead taken sometimes by one and sometimes by the other.

That skills in reading and writing are closely related is an educational commonplace. Observational studies of young children by Durkin (1966), Read (1970), Clay (1975), and Clark (1976) all confirm that reading and spelling develop together though not necessarily simultaneously. Durkin's and Clark's early readers were also "paper and pencil kids," and Clay reports that spelling ability is the best indicator of begin-

ning reading skill. We have less information on the exact
nature of the reading-spelling relationship. Read, who noted
that "all the spontaneous spellers learned to read with little formal instruction" (1970, p. 185), further observed that most of
his children learned to spell *before* reading, some coincidentally
with reading. Though their spellings matured as their reading
became more skillful, he noted that their spelling development
and reading development were "not parallel in detail" (p. 183).
These are patterns I observed in Paul's development.

Paul's invented spelling developed rapidly (during six
months) to a point where he could without help transcribe to
his own satisfaction any word in his vocabulary, such as
IKSPLOSIVS (5:7) and DRAKSHINS (5:8). His reading required more practice and took longer to develop to the point
where he could use it on his own. In writing and spelling, Paul
showed great persistence and effort over relatively short spans
of time (weeks or months). His reading seemed to develop
more casually but with steady interest over a longer span
(many months) and with less frequent bursts of concentrated
effort.

Paul's sense of correctness or of the units of correspondence
between print and speech was not parallel for his reading and
writing. During his rehearsing reading phase, the units of
correspondence were the book and the story, the picture and
the events it depicted in the story sequence. By the time Paul
started spelling inventively, he tacitly conceived of reading as
being based on precise print-speech relationships. He seemed
to know that the printed word stood for only one word, which
was either read correctly or not, and he responded to this need
for correctness by not reading aloud until sure he was correct
(silences), asking for words, and somewhat later by laboriously
sounding out hard words. At the same time, the unit of correctness in his spelling was the letter-sound relationship; his questions were about how to represent speech sounds, not how to
spell words. It was his reading, I assume, that helped him move
toward standard spelling and a sense of correctness in spelling
words, first evidenced at 5:8. Several months later, as his
reading was increasing speed, he let phonic approximations of
unfamiliar words stand as place holders, in the interests of

understanding a unit larger than the word—phrases, sentences, groups of sentences.

Paul did not tacitly conceive of reading as merely the converse of writing; that is, as decoding letters to sounds. As evident from his errors, questions, and frequent comments about the content while reading, his early reading was more a search for meaning than a search for sounds. I have mentioned a few instances where he had difficulty decoding words as a result of applying his own phonic overgeneralizations that consonant letters have a unique sound (*s* always sounds like "s") and that letters are always pronounced (final *e*). Since scattered instances like these stand out in my records, it would seem that in reading Paul was not just applying *his* system. He was also able to read correctly words (such as "fair") that he would have spelled otherwise (FAR). Read, too, noted that his inventive spellers "could usually read words in standard orthography that they continued to spell differently" (1970, p. 183). This may be because consonants, which inventive spellers usually represent quite conventionally, convey more information about most English words than do vowels. Consonants are more frequent than vowels in most words, appear most often in the prominent initial and final positions in words, represent a greater number and variety of speech sounds, and have more predictable sound-letter relationships. Compare the consonant patterns in Paul's invented spelling at 5:6 with the similar consonant patterns in a conventional spelling of the same statement:

H-- T- D- TH- -ND-N W-R D-NS (invented spelling)
H-- T- D- TH -ND--N W-R D-NC- (conventional spelling)
(How to do the Indian war dance)

In contrast, Paul's vowel representations are unlike the vowels in a conventional spelling of that statement:

-AU -O -O -- E--E- -O- -A-- (invented spelling)
-OW -O -O --E I--IA- -A- -A--E (conventional spelling)

Because English has so many more vowel sounds than vowel letters, each letter must serve to represent more than one vowel sound. Operationally Paul understood this very early in his spelling development but only months later in reading. When

he reached the stage in decoding of trying out alternative pronunciations if the first one did not sound right to him, he
located vowels as the letters whose sounds were variable and
experimented with a selection of alternative sounds.

When Paul was 5:7 I noted a difference between his spelling
and reading strategies. Except for a few memorized words, he
spelled by sounding out and often syllabifying as part of that
process. His reading did not proceed in a letter-by-letter or
syllable-by-syllable sounding-out process. He was aided by advance expectations of what the words said—not yet context
clues from the reading itself, but external context clues; for example, seeing the cottage cheese in the container or recognizing
the container and then reading the label, or having heard
something read to him before he tried reading it. When he was
5:11 I again noted a difference. From his invented spelling it
was clear that Paul had the ability to analyze and remember
sound sequences. It would therefore seem that he could read by
sounding out letters and blending them. Perhaps he *could,* but
that was not his strategy. He used phonic clues—paid attention
to letter-sound relationships—but seemed to perceive words
more holistically, and thus letters sometimes got out of order
("flood" for "fold," "inspycrot" for "inspector").

In a broader sense, Paul's spelling and reading were related,
for sounding out spellings for his messages and reading his own
writings were practice with fundamental principles of reading:
that the letters on the page stand for the sounds and thus the
words and meanings of the spoken language. In his first year of
reading, as in invented spelling, Paul essentially regarded each
word as a new problem; he was reinventing and redecoding,
not memorizing sight or spelling words. He took an active,
problem-solving approach to print, as young children do in
learning the rules of their spoken language.

Paul learned to read music as he learned to read words—by
writing as much as by reading. Perhaps I was influenced by
having observed his learning to read and write when I suggested that he try writing down familiar tunes he had picked
out on the piano. With my help he did so, learning notation by
a "music experience" approach when he was eight years old. "I
never thought I'd be able to read music!" he exclaimed in

amazement and delight—but he went no further with music at the time, as though the competence rather than continued use was what mattered. At nine years he started recorder lessons, and almost at once his teacher asked him to compose simple rounds and duets, the forms of music that he was also reading. Of course this method was determined by his teacher, but its success and Paul's enthusiasm were *his* response.

Perhaps the broadest relationship between his early development in reading and that in writing is their common basis in metalinguistic functioning. Paul's invented spellings were one expression of metalinguistic awareness; to spell inventively a child must think about, analyze, and isolate the sounds of his language. Paul's knowledge of word boundaries was expressed graphically by dots or spaces as well as recognized in reading. Understanding what reading involves means understanding the often arbitrary, conventional relations between the patterns of spoken and written language. This requires a higher level of consciousness about language than the recognition of sight words or spelling by rote. Perhaps this higher metalinguistic awareness is the dividing line between Biemiller's context-dependent and graphic-information-using readers.

Research on children's metalinguistic awareness, though initiated before 1970, has increased during the period of research on invented spelling; however, little explicit connection has been made between the two. Cazden points out that Read's research "suggests that individual differences may be greater in metalinguistic awareness than in language ability per se" (Cazden, 1972, p. 87).

In her review of studies on metalinguistic awareness, Ryan states that "as a deliberate language activity, reading may require a degree of linguistic awareness not necessary for speaking and listening effectively in everyday interactions"; and in her conclusion she urges directing major research efforts toward "illuminating the relation between a young child's reading level and his ability in metalinguistic tasks which demand various levels of awareness" (Ryan, forthcoming). One such study by Irving (1975) found that a high-middle-low group stratification of twenty-eight first graders based on teacher evaluation of their reading performance corresponded with their stratification as measured by success on a variety of metalinguistic tasks encompassing sound, meaning, and structure. The best readers were also the best metalinguists, and so on down. A comment by Clay from her classroom observation of beginning readers supports Irving's findings: "It was a surprise to me to find children playfully creating contrasts between shapes, meanings, sounds and word patterns. The examples come *only from those children who made rapid progress in learning to read,* but they are further evidence of the urge not only to explore, but also to order one's knowledge" (Clay, 1975, p. 37; emphasis added).

Most important, the present case study, along with other studies of invented spelling and beginning reading strategies as seen through analysis of errors, reveals the dynamic nature of children's learning about written language. Children do not seem to accumulate discrete bits of information and correct habits but rather to evolve increasingly efficient — that is, comprehensive, informed, and practiced — strategies for understanding the relations between spoken and written language. Children begin reading and spelling with oversimplified or incomplete notions of what each involves. The research of both Biemiller and Clay suggests that beginning reading achievement is correlated with a child's ability to *change* his strategies. Progress toward standard spelling, as Read and others have shown, is made through changes in children's categorizations. As children take into account more kinds of information, their reading and spelling become more accurate. "Learning to read and to write are matters of knowledge rather than habit" (Read, 1971, p. 34). What is educationally important, then, is extending and revising children's knowledge about how written language works.

As he moved from the sound transcription approach of invented spelling toward standard spelling, Paul not only conventionalized his sound-letter relationships but also showed an increasing awareness of the complexity and indirectness of sound-spelling patterns: he had a larger repertoire of conventional alternatives for representing sounds, showed awareness of environmental constraints, and spelled conventionally an increasing number of morphemes (the smallest meaningful units of language, including roots, affixes, and inflections). Each word was no longer a new problem in sound transcription. More and more spellings became automatic; those he had to figure out showed strategies involving letter groups rather than letter-by-letter (or sound-by-sound) construction — word *parts* were becoming familiar. He attempted to correct spelling errors he perceived by trying out alternative spellings and seeing which one looked right. His concept of spelling changed, and though he still used letter-sound relationships, this strategy was subordinated to visual (recall) and semantic (morphemic) strategies within his expanded understanding of the nature of our spelling system. The visual and morphemic were the new branches of his continued growth in spelling.

Paul's increasing fluency in reading also was an outgrowth of the differentiation and integration of several strategies, decoding and contextual, which facilitated self-corrections and reading in units increasingly larger than single words. He let phonic approximations (nonsense words) stand as place holders to get on with the sentence. In both spelling and reading, his knowledge of a wide range of morphemes, especially Latinate ones, was evident.

spelling (9:8)	*reading (9:5)*
commercialization	nichrome
intergalactic	electr — electromagnetic
reincarnation	depósit-chon (deposition)
informative	thermodynamic
combustable	audiable (audible)
collapsable	aimable (amiable)

The spelling words were of his own choosing; the reading words were from a list. "Audible" is apparently still an unfamiliar word here, but he comes a lot closer to its morphemes than he did in oral reading at 7:5 with "addidoobullen-doo-bul-bul-bul." He does not see *-ible* as an alternative form of *-able*. His misstressing "deposition" shows at least his recognition of familiar elements in an unfamiliar word. As his decoding and spelling skills became more and more automatic, reading and writing were less effortful and he could focus almost entirely on content.

From the beginning Paul's writing was influenced by his reading in many ways. He learned much of his spelling and some vocabulary through reading. He learned most of his punctuation and other writing conventions from reading. He learned forms and styles of written language from reading. Or rather, he learned by practicing in his writing things he had observed in reading; he learned to write by writing as well as by reading. Because he was so actively and continuously engaged in writing, he may have paid more attention to some things in reading that answered questions he had as a writer.

In following the evolution of Paul's newspapers and his turn to magazine production, we have seen the influence of reading on the forms, content, spatial arrangements, and style of his writing. Precursors of his full-blown literary imitation of science fiction writing go back more than five years to his signs (MAN WRKEN WETH BLOKS) and "shopping lists" (5000 BATLZ.AV.WESKY., and so on), to the introduction he adapted for his "Fun Book" when he was seven ("This is not a regular book if you want to you can skip to the middle or somewhere near the end or you can just work your way through anyway it's fun"), and to the bookish language of some of his school writing the following years ("A prism is a thick (mostly) peice of glass that puts the colors of sunlight visible to the human eye," written at 8:7).

Are children who are avid readers more advanced in their writing abilities than children who read little? Are children who write prolifically better writers than those who write little, regardless of amount of reading? What kinds of things do children learn about writing from reading, and what kinds of information require direct instruction? We do not know yet, but we need to know.

Britton (1970a) sees the earliest influence of reading on writing in terms of the poems and stories children have heard read aloud to them. Beyond that stage he sees more diverse literary influences as children's individually selected models affect their writing. "As the influence of the written language increases, their progress in writing depends more and more on the nature of the reading input" (Britton, 1970a, p. 38).

Reading seems to have had a broader influence on Paul's

writing from the beginning than it did on the writing of the children Britton observed. Harste and his colleagues (forthcoming) have demonstrated preschoolers' awareness of print as they interpret signs, labels, and advertisements. Such forms were important models for Paul's early writings. The models he selected changed over time, as did the nature of the influence of reading on his writing; consider the shift from signs and labels to *Battlestar Galactica.* Carol Chomsky (1972) has demonstrated a strong correlation between reading exposure, including being read aloud to, and language development. Although she tested oral language comprehension, there is no reason to assume that written language development would not also be advanced.

If reading provides models, however unconsciously used, for children's writing, then the kinds of reading children are exposed to take on additional educational importance. Britton urges us to "consider on the one hand the range of writing tasks for which children need to prepare, and on the other hand the very limited resources available to them as input—as for example in their scientific or geographical or historical studies . . . The models of such writing to be found in school textbooks are very far from adequate" (Britton, 1970b, p. 38).

Finally, for Paul, writing and reading were related through their meanings to him as a person—through their appeal to and development of his interests, his character, his style. These personal continuities emerge over several years of observations. Some of Paul's interests—such as jokes, riddles, magic, and science fiction—are common to many children; they are unique only in their particular interaction with his personality.

Paul's first choice of reading material that was significantly different from what had been read aloud to him was joke and riddle books. The *Nitty-Gritty Rhyming Riddle Book* was the first book he sat down to struggle through when he was just beginning to read. Other joke and riddle books followed in the next few years. *Bert's Hall of Great Inventions,* a particular favorite of his, combined humor and inventions. During his second year of writing he wrote jokes and riddles; later he preferred just to tell them, and his humor came to include much punning. His riddles—spoken and written—were sometimes serious, connecting with his mathematical or scientific interests: "What was once a rock but without the ocean it wouldn't be smaller than you are?" (6:6). The answer is sand.

Paul's delight in inventions has been expressed in an increasing variety of ways since early childhood: building constructions with blocks and other materials; drawing complicated machines; rereading innumerable times *Bert's Hall of Great Inventions* and later reading stories about young inventors and scientists; giving detailed explanations of how things work, both orally and in his writings (like step-by-step directions accompanying his constructions, and explanations in his "Magic Carpet" story); and devising his own experiments and constructions from kits rather than following the printed instructions. This last approach was also evident in his schoolwork when he altered directions in workbook sorts of assignments for himself. (What I call "inventiveness" a teacher might well call "not following directions.") An elaborative style in his approach to doing things—as in making up tales to accompany some of his magic tricks in performance—seems a further expession of his inventiveness.

Attention to details was evident in Paul's drawings, in his care in explaining and describing things in his writing, and in his interest in details in reading and especially rereading books. The high point of this tendency was his absorption in every detail of *Star Wars*. Without his detailed awareness of syntax and punctuation, he could not have successfully imitated professional science fiction writing in "The Death of Starbuck."

Expressiveness characterized his speech intonations as well as his oral reading. He carried this expressiveness over into his handwriting by varying the size and texture of letters for dramatic effect and by his generous use of exclamation points. Although such graphic dynamics were most prominent in his earlier writings after he had become an independent inventive speller, they persisted in his signs and flourished again in *Strange* magazine.

These characteristics lose their life as they are abstracted and itemized. They distinguish Paul only in their interconnectedness, which may be seen if the reader looks again, with them in mind at Paul's "Magic Carpet" story (pp. 75-78). A pervasive concern in that story is "control," which is related to the playful mastery of his inventiveness and to his persistence and determination in completing to his satisfaction tasks *he* set for himself. The periods of great concentration that characterized his early reading and especially his writing development also involved great frustration and often tears at interruptions and errors. This sort of potentially explosive concentration and setting high standards for himself continued to characterize his periods of intense work on other things.

Time allows such continuities and recurrences — as well as the transformations — to stand out, while it blurs cause and effect by the uncontrolled accumulation of many variables. But perhaps cause and effect in the life of a person are not easy to assess anyway. As Robert White has observed, "Many forces operate at once in a given personality, producing an elaborate lattice of interconnected events rather than a simple model of cause and effect" (1952, pp. 327-328). Looking closely at an individual confronts us with the lattice, and with the limits of our categorical knowing and explaining.

When he was five and a half years old, Paul wrote and posted this sign over his workbench-desk: DO NAT DSTRB GNYS AT WRK. The GNYS (genius) at work is our human capacity for language. DO NAT DSTRB is a caution to observe how it works, for the logic by which we teach is not always the logic by which children learn.

Learning to Write and Read as Forms of Development

16

In looking at an individual human being in the act of learning particular things, we are also seeing beyond that individual and beyond the particulars he is learning. What does Paul's learning to write and read mean not just for children's literacy learning, not just for education, but for understanding ourselves as human beings?

Learning to write and read are processes shaped by more comprehensive patterns of human growth and learning: the acquisition of universals before culture-specifics, development from global to differentiated and integrated functioning, and movement outward beyond the immediate in time and space and beyond our personal perspective—what Piaget has called "decentration." Although reading and writing have long been associated with teaching and instruction, this and other studies of preschoolers show that children learn more about print and learn it earlier than they are taught. In a literate society, learning to write and read may be natural. In the broadest sense of the words, "writing" (including drawing) and "reading" (including interpreting visual aspects of the world besides print) are universal; and learning to write and read share in those basic processes by which we grow as human beings.

Pattern 1: From Universals to Culture-Specifics

Children learn first those aspects of language that are most universal and last those that are most culture-specific. This pattern was formulated and documented for phonological development by Jakobson, who related "individual linguistic competence to the structural principles of the languages of the world" (1968, p. 65). Born with the capacity to learn any of the world's languages, children in all cultures learn first the universal consonant-vowel distinction, which is fundamental to all language systems.

> At the beginning of the first stage of language development, the acquisition of vowels is launched with a wide vowel, and, at the same time, the acquisition of consonants by a forward articulated stop. An *a* emerges as the first vowel, and generally a labial as the first consonant, in child language. The first consonantal opposition is that of nasal and oral stop (e.g., mama-papa), which is followed by the opposition of labials and dentals (e.g., papa-tata and mama-nana). These two oppositions form the minimal consonantal system of the languages of the world. These are the only oppositions that cannot be lacking anywhere. (Jakobson, 1968, pp. 47-48)

Universal features are fundamental because they form the foundation upon which finer, culture-specific distinctions are built. "Both the ontogeny and, probably, the phylogeny of language are based on the same underlying principle, which governs the whole realm of language. This principle is simple to the point of being trivial: one cannot erect the superstructure without having provided the foundation nor can one remove the foundation without having removed the superstructure" (Jakobson, 1968, p. 93).

In the realm of art, young children's drawings have been found to be similar across cultures (Kellogg, 1969). Representations of people and houses, which might be expected to reflect cultural differences, are remarkably uniform. Children's pictorial art, in Kellogg's analysis, develops out of their abstract shapes rather than from close observation of the objects they depict. Abstract art, she reminds us, precedes pictorial art in the history of the human race as well as in the development of the individual. As summarized by Herbert Read, Kellogg's theory is that "every child, in its discovery of a mode of symbolization, follows the same graphic evolution. Out of the amorphous scribblings of the infant emerge, first certain basic forms, the circle, the upright cross, the diagonal cross, the rectangle, etc., and then two or more of these basic forms are combined into that comprehensive symbol known as the *mandala,* a circle divided into quarters by a cross . . . The process . . . is universal and is found not only in the scribblings of children but everywhere where the making of signs has had a symbolizing purpose—which is from the Neolithic Age onwards" (quoted by Kellogg, 1969, p. 2).

These universal or archetypal forms are the foundation upon which the superstructures of art and writing are built. Although the close relationship between drawing and writing is a commonplace in histories of writing systems, our society regards drawing so much as pictorial and writing so much as phonetic that the relation between the two is less evident to adults than to children, who are not yet as fully acculturated. A recent study (Schmandt-Besserat, 1978) argues that the earliest writing evolved not from pictures but from abstract shapes. "Most of the letters of the English alphabet, both capitals and lowercase forms, are made by young children as art Gestalts. In art, the letters are placed or arranged to complete a Pattern or an implied shape. In language, the letters are arranged in a certain order within words and are put into certain left-right and top-bottom placement" (Kellogg, 1969, p. 262). Thus one of the first things a child needs to learn in school as a writer, she argues, is the difference between the use of letter shapes for art and for language.

If ontogeny recapitulates phylogeny it is not because primitive or ancient people were childish but because what is fundamental, perhaps to the point of being innately human, develops first. Learning universals first ensures that the maximum number of options remains available for the greatest flexibility in development. Further and further distinctions and complexities do not represent the only form of progress, as Wolf (1977) has demonstrated in his analysis of the historical recurrence of simpler though different artistic styles following the development to extreme complexity of musical, literary, and graphic art styles.

Language and art are not only culturally transmitted; they are also reinvented by children, who increasingly shape their inventions to cultural forms. "Children have real understanding only of that which they invent themselves, and each time we try to teach them something too quickly, we keep them from reinventing it for themselves" (Piaget as quoted by C. Chomsky, 1974, pp. 13-14). Kellogg, from her twenty-year study of children's drawings, has observed "basic Gestalts . . . reborn in the minds of each generation in childhood" (1969, p. 215). Chukovsky reports instances of young children reinventing archaic language forms. The child's mind "masters, as if miraculously, the same methods, processes, and peculiarities of word construction which were used by his very distant ancestors in building the language" (Chukovsky, 1971, p. 5). Reinvention is not unique to individual development; it has also occurred in human history, for example, with the independent invention of writing systems.

What is fundamental and universal in writing and reading? Writing is a symbol system conveying a stable verbal message; reading is deciphering such a message from graphic symbols. If writing has its roots in drawing, then children's early "reading" from pictures is a basic form of reading. Writing systems can be basically phonetic or nonphonetic. Historically and for the child, the earliest writings interpreted and created are nonphonetic: pictographic and ideographic scripts for mankind, pictures and scribbles for children. Phonetic writing systems are syllabic or alphabetic (a later development), with the alphabetic further differentiated into systems that represent mainly consonants and those that represent all vowels as well as consonants. Looking back at Paul's development as a writer and reader, we can see him moving through such a historical pattern of development from universals to increasingly culture-specific distinctions.

Paul's first readings were from pictures in books and later from signs that he recognized but did not decode phonetically. His first messages were letter forms in somewhat nonlinear arrangement, designed to fit the shape of the paper—in that sense more like Kellogg's art Gestalts; but like writing, they were intended to convey a verbal message. When he started inventing spellings Paul knew that writing (in English) was phonetic, though his first spellings were a combination of syllabic and alphabetic. (Historically, pure writing systems are rare.) He also knew the spatial arrangement of letter forms in writing: linear, left to right for his language. He could conceivably have written right to left or plough-wise (alternately from right to left and from left to right), options chosen by other cultures whose writing has the same linear appearance as ours. Serpentine and columnar writing are further spatial options that have been used in other times and places, and Graves (1979b) has shown a first grader who wrote words in a column. Paul drew from this cross-cultural pool of options for written language when he reinvented the dot system to separate words. Some of the things children do in writing and reading may appear less strange to us if we are aware of systems used by other cultures, systems that children are free to reinvent. From this perspective, cross-cultural and historical studies of writing and reading may be significant for understanding children's written language behavior.

Pattern 2: From Global to Differentiated and Integrated Functioning

Development is contrasted to mere changes over time by Werner and Kaplan, who argue that "organisms are naturally directed towards a series of transformations—reflecting a tendency to move from a state of relative globality and undifferentiatedness toward states of increasing differentiation and hierarchic integration" (1963, p. 152). This increase of differentiation and hierarchic integration is seen by Werner (1948) as the fundamental law of development. It is a law derived from biology, where

> development is seen as continual *differentiation:* over time, if conditions are suitable, a diffuse whole of a given size and shape decomposes into parts of more specific form and function. (For instance, over the first four weeks of life, initially identical cells

give rise to a separate head, tail, heart, liver, and gastrointestinal tract.) But even as development involves differentiation, it also entails *integration:* Parts that were once isolated come together to form a new, better organized system. (For instance, in the newborn, there is little coordination between seeing, hearing, and moving; but in the infant of six months or a year, considerable integration of these components proves the rule.) Thus as different parts of the body become interconnected, the result is a more flexible organism. (Gardner, 1978, p. 248)

This pattern of development from global to differentiated and integrated functioning has been observed in language learning, for example by Lefevre:

> There is ample evidence to establish the primacy of large, overriding general patterns in the early language learning of infants and young children. These patterns are sentences and sentence-like structures, delineated and shaped by basic patterns of native English melodies and rhythms . . . And while these fundamental structural patterns of intonation may be accompanied by expressive features that are entirely optional, this fact should not obscure the systematic use of the underlying patterns, which are not only of fundamental importance in English language structure, but of prior occurrence in the native language learning process. *Intonation precedes the development of the phonemic repertoire and the formation of vocabulary:* indeed, preschool children often cannot single out so-called words from longer utterances. (Lefevre, 1973, p. 297)

The development of Paul's reading and spelling skills follows the basic developmental pattern of differentiation and integration. "Relative globality" was evident in his "reading" the Curious George story from the pictures, and in the welcome home banner with letterlike forms that he "wrote" for me. Clay has observed about learning to write that "the first things learnt will be *gross approximations* which later become refined: weird letter forms, invented words, make-believe sentences" (1975, p. 15). Beginnings involve global and imprecise strategies and understandings. From a developmental view, correctness is not the first stage but a later refinement of initial approximations. Reading and spelling are both tasks requiring precise performance, but this is not necessarily achieved by trying to insist on precision from the start.

A global awareness provides a framework within which the differentiated specifics function and have meaning. Thus children's early rehearsals or pretend versions of reading and writing establish the context in which details, such as letter-sound correspondences, can be meaningful. As specific features of print and strategies for responding to them are increasingly differentiated, these are integrated into a hierarchic structure governed by broad concepts about print and by purposes in reading and writing. As Moffett (1968) has argued, the "particle approach" in teaching, which builds from the smallest to the largest units (as from letters to words to sentences in writing or reading), does not reflect either the way the language or the minds of children function.

The history of Paul's learning to write and read was one of "increasing differentiation" and "hierarchic integration." He moved from associating letter forms in general with meaning (as on his banner) to associating specific letter forms with specific speech sounds. Once he mastered an invented spelling system that transcribed speech phonemically, he became aware of other bases for spelling, and focused on units larger than phonemes—on words and on morphemes. Before these differentiated aspects of spelling became integrated, there was some interference between concepts, as in Paul's spelling of "the" as TEH from visual recall after he had mastered the digraph *th* in invented spelling. Later, he was able to coordinate phonic principles, visual recall, and morphemic awareness to help determine spellings he was uncertain about or to correct misspellings. Use of more than a single strategy provides a basis for self-corrections in spelling, as in reading. Paul seemed to be asking himself not only, "What does this word *sound* like?" and "What does this word *look* like?" but "What does it *mean*?" As he grew aware of more variant spelling patterns, he also grew more aware of the conditions (such as position in word) governing the choice among those possibilities. Operationally, he was aware of the complex nature of our orthography.

In reviewing the evolution of two persistent forms in Paul's writing, newspapers and stories, we saw the development of increasingly complex and differentiated structures, such as more diverse sections in newspapers and more complicated plots and varied settings in stories. From an initial declaratory style, Paul diversified into dialogue and narration, eventually differentiating the narrator from himself.

In reading, Paul moved from the gross correspondences of story sequence with picture sequence to differentiating finer correspondences of printed to spoken word, and letter to sound. Later, in revising decoded words that did not sound right to him, he distinguished letters with frequently varied pronunciations (vowels and consonants such as *c* and *g*) from letters with more stable pronunciations (many consonants). His ability to self-correct errors in reading resulted from his integration of various reading strategies—use of letter-sound, syntactic, and semantic cues. By age seven his purposes became more diverse: to practice decoding on harder materials, to gain speed on easy materials and expressiveness in reading aloud familiar books; to enjoy the sounds of poems. He varied his reading according to the type of material and his purpose in reading it.

"Development is not a matter of cumulatively taking in outside information," nor does it mean "the disappearance of the old scheme and the simple substitution of a new scheme. Rather, organic development implies a progressive structuring so that later structures subsume earlier structures on a new level of functioning" (Furth, 1970, pp. 41-42). Not just information, but the *organization* of information is crucial to cognitive development. Paul did not, for instance, discard all he had learned about phonics from invented spelling when he moved on; it was relativized and qualified within the context of a more complex and comprehensive view of spelling. "Every shift involves the relativizing of what was taken as ultimate" (Kegan, 1977, p. 244).

The growth of Paul's spelling and reading skills can be seen through a developmental psychologist's view as cognitive systems increasing in complexity and structural differentiation. This increasing complexity means that the child can move away from earlier oversimplifications and come closer to grasping the actual complexity of our orthography. Complexity also allows more room for growth within a scheme so that qualitative changes occur less and less frequently.

Adults can supply children with the information for cumulative learning within schemes or concepts, but who generates
the revolutions? They may even go relatively unnoticed, as
Kuhn, who has analyzed "paradigm shifts" on a grander scale,
pointed out: "Scientific revolutions . . . need seem revolutionary only to those whose paradigms are affected by them.
To outsiders they may . . . seem normal parts of the developmental process" (Kuhn, 1970, pp. 92-93). Through an adult
perspective, children's learning may appear cumulative; from a
child's view it may seem revolutionary.

Both the closeness of my view and its extension over time
necessarily make my interpretation of Paul's learning quite different from that of a teacher working with him among a group
of children for nine or ten months. Because of the way most
schools are set up, with sizable groups of children moving year-
ly from teacher to teacher, development — which really requires
a longer view, especially after first grade when changes are apt
to slow down — is hard to see. The qualitative changes that are
part of that growth as well as the continuities that are part of
the person may not emerge, and yet these factors may be the
most important ones for motivating and assessing a child's
learning.

An understanding of qualitative changes in learning may be
more helpful for teachers than quantitative measures, especially in aiding the development of children who are having difficulties. My experience in teaching such children is that their
quantitatively slow progress is associated with limited strategies
and concepts in reading and writing — with qualitative im-
mobility. Bruner, in commenting on the qualitative changes of
skill that mark progress points in development, adds: "The difference between 'good skiing' and 'bad skiing' is, alas,
qualitative, not quantitative" (1969, p. 176). So is the difference between good and poor reading or writing.

Pattern 3: Decentration

The world of a 4- or 5-year-old is typically a world of nearness
to hand, a world bound together by feeling, in which things
exist only in their immediate meaning for the child . . . From
our observation, this world begins to break up some time be-

tween 6-8, and the source of the break-up also presages the
emergent interests of the child during the later primary and elementary years. As the young child plays, as he forms, con-
structs, draws, and names the things of the world, he is in the
process of separating himself from the objects and the objects
from him. As the things of the world gain stability, they begin
to stand apart from him and his feeling. Standing apart, they
become things in their own right to be explored in a whole
variety of ways. (Carini, 1973, p. 13)

When Paul was seven and a half and we were on an airplane
trip, tuning in and out of the radio programs for passengers,
Paul commented that he used to think that when he shut off the
television and then turned it on later, he would get the show at
the point where he had shut it off. His earlier view that the program (and earlier still, that the world) did not exist independently of him characterizes what Piaget has called
egocentrism. Paul's awareness of the television program's existence apart from his watching it illustrates what Piaget has
called decentration — movement away from an egocentric view
of the world.

> [Piaget] describes children as *egocentric* — not because they think
> a lot about themselves, but rather because children are in-
> capable of separating their own perspective from that of other
> people. In fact, nearly all of Piaget's several dozen books can be
> read as a lengthy account of the child's slow growth out of
> egocentrism — a gradual *decentration* as the child becomes able to
> represent how the world looks to other people and how those
> views differ from her own. And, in a similar spirit, the egocen-
> tric infant can be seen as attributing all consequences to her
> own behavior, only gradually coming to recognize a world
> apart from her own actions and conceptions. (Gardner, 1978,
> p. 63)

Decentration involves differentiating oneself from other per-
sons and objects, and thus becoming conscious of oneself; it
also involves, through the growth of memory and language, extending and differentiating apprehensions of time and space
beyond the immediate — to past and future, and existent but
elsewhere. The expansiveness of decentration was evident as
Paul grew interested in reading information about the world at

large, became conscious of an audience as he wrote, sustained the reading or writing of a work over days or weeks, and extended the plots and settings of his stories through space and time. Reaching beyond the near and immediate, Paul encompassed more of the world, becoming more knowledgeable and also more objective as he acknowledged its separateness from him.

Paul's expanding awareness of the world and his growing capacities for interacting with it verbally are reflected in his writing. The process of knowing his world and distinguishing it from himself that he expressed earlier through naming things with spoken language, he continued through writing signs, labels, and captions when he was five years old. As his reasoning developed, in the next year or two, his charts and other organizational writings that categorized the things he knew extended his intellectual control of the world. Imaginatively, he dealt with this now separate world through stories that confronted characters (often himself and his friends) with unusual adventures and challenges. The world within himself became separate enough for him to describe it in diaries. He became aware of how much there was to learn about the world outside. He also came to feel the power such knowledge conferred, as expressed in his "Know-It All" book.

In Paul's early writing there was no clear distinction between writer and audience. Moving outward from an egocentric view of the world, he became conscious of audience, of what needed to be explained to someone else. In "A Magic Carpet or Two" we are aware of the storyteller as well as the story — a storyteller with control of his material, a sense of humor, and awareness of his audience. Mindful that a reader might have questions about some characters and events in the story, Paul addressed himself, at times explicitly, to those questions (for example, "two of my best friends Kenny and Matthew" and "I suppose you want to know how you steer a magic carpet"). He could stand outside his understanding of what he had written. Such a growing awareness of audience in young writers of this age (Paul was eight) has been noted by Graves (1978). Flavell's research (1968) indicates that the ability to take another person's awareness into account begins to increase at about age seven.

Paul not only distinguished himself from his audience, but also differentiated a widening circle of audiences: parents, peers, teachers, and strangers. His writing style was modified according to his audience as well as according to the increasingly differentiated forms in which he wrote. "Differentiating among modes of discourse, registers of speech, kinds of audiences is essentially a matter of decentering, of seeing alternatives, of standing in others' shoes, of knowing that one has a private or local point of view and knowledge structure" (Moffett, 1968, p. 57).

With the creation of "Pistol Paul" at eight years old, Paul began to role-play through writing. At ten he created the character of himself as editor of *Strange* magazine and stylistically assumed the voice of a professional science fiction writer. "Acting a role, realizing in a special way one's identity (in a sense) with someone who (in another sense) one is not, remains one of the most human things a man can do. No brute animal can act a role. Unable to recognize himself, he finds it impossible to recognize what by contrast with self is other. By the same token, he has nothing against which to set a role so that it is a role" (Walter J. Ong as quoted by Gibson, 1969, p. 85). The distancing from self that is self-consciousness is another aspect of decentration.

Acknowledging and bridging the separateness of others seems a lifelong learning process for all of us who are beyond childhood—as teachers, friends, partners, and members of families. The history of science, too, is a history of decentering, of moving away from an anthropocentric view of the universe, and more recently, as we appreciate its ecology and autonomy, acknowledging the limits to our ability to control that separate world for our own purposes.

While learning to write and learning to read are part of the broad patterns of growth this chapter has focused on—acquisition of universals before culture-specifics, development from global to differentiated functioning, and decentration—they also have distinct patterns and purposes of their own. And each individual who learns to write and read, in an environmental interaction that is never identical with any other's, adapts these patterns and purposes uniquely.

Paul's writing and reading did not "just grow." "Growth in a given direction takes place under certain conditions and through certain types of experience. It is not just something that happens because we grow older" (White, 1952, p. 332). In detailing this history of Paul, I hope the conditions and experiences that nurtured his growth are visible. Some I may have taken so for granted that I neglected to point them out.

Though Paul was surrounded by many potential influences, he necessarily responded to only some of them. He was in control of his own learning, seeking out certain information and experiences, ignoring or avoiding others; and so, although he was not in control of his own environment, he acted on it.

There is always more than one way to look at a collection of data. I hope I have presented enough raw material for the reader's understanding to be enriched by his own interpretations. I hope, too, that this study may help other children to be seen more clearly in their own right as learners.

References

Index

References

Barr, R. 1974-75. The effect of instruction on pupil reading strategies. *Reading Research Quarterly* 4:555-582.

Beers, J. W., and Henderson, E. H. 1977. A study of developing orthographic concepts among first graders. *Research in the Teaching of English* 11: 133-148.

Biemiller, A. 1970. The development of the use of graphic and contextual information as children learn to read. *Reading Research Quarterly* 6:75-96.

Blackie, J. 1971. *Inside the primary school.* New York: Schocken.

Britton, J. 1970a. *Language and learning.* Coral Gables, Fla.: University of Miami Press.

————1970b. The student's writing. In *Explorations in children's writing,* ed. E. L. Evertts. Urbana, Ill.: National Council of Teachers of English.

Bruner, J. S. 1969. On voluntary action and its hierarchical structure. In *Beyond reductionism,* ed. A. Koestler and J. R. Smythies. New York: Macmillan.

Burgess, C., et al. 1973. *Understanding children writing.* Harmondsworth, England: Penguin Education.

Carini, P. 1973. Child development: A basis for open classroom curriculum. Speech at Cortland College Conference, May 1973 (mimeo).

Cazden, C. B. 1972. *Child language and education.* New York: Holt, Rinehart and Winston.

Chall, J. 1979. The great debate: Ten years later, with a modest proposal for reading stages. In *Theory and practice of early reading,* vol. 1, ed. L. B. Resnick and P. A. Weaver. Hillsdale, N.J.: Erlbaum.

Chomsky, C. 1970. Reading, writing, and phonology. *Harvard Educational Review* 40:287-309.

————1971a. Write first, read later. *Childhood Education* 47:296-299.

————1971b. Invented spelling in the open classroom. *Word* 27:1-3.

————1972. Stages in language development and reading exposure. *Harvard Educational Review* 42:1-33.

————1974. Invented spelling in first grade. Harvard Graduate School of Education (mimeo).

————1976. Approaching reading through invented spelling. Paper prepared for the Conference on Beginning Reading Instruction, University of Pittsburgh, May 1976.

CHUKOVSKY, K. 1971. *From two to five,* ed. and trans. M. Morton, Berkeley, Calif.: University of California Press. (Originally published in 1925.)

CLARK, M. M. 1976. *Young fluent readers.* London: Heinemann.

CLAY, M. 1966. The reading behaviour of 5 year old children: A research report. *New Zealand Journal of Educational Studies* 2:11-31.

————1969. Reading errors and self-correction behaviour. *British Journal of Educational Psychology* 30:47-56.

————1972. *Reading: The patterning of complex behaviour.* London: Heinemann.

————1975. *What did I write?* Auckland, New Zealand: Heinemann.

COOK, L. D. 1978. Test report on JA. Harvard Graduate School of Education (unpublished report).

DI LEO, J. H. 1977. *Child development: Analysis and synthesis.* New York: Brunner/Mazel.

DUCKWORTH, E. 1973. Language and thought. In *Piaget in the classroom,* ed. M. Schwebel and J. Raph. New York: Basic Books.

DURKIN, D. 1966. *Children who read early.* New York: Teachers College Press.

EDUCATIONAL TESTING SERVICE, EARLY EDUCATION RESEARCH GROUP. *Collaborative research project on reading.* Princeton, N.J. (unpublished reports).

FLAVELL, J. H., et al. 1968. *The development of role-taking and communication skills in children.* New York: Wiley.

FURTH, H. G. 1970. *Piaget for teachers.* Englewood Cliffs, N.J.: Prentice-Hall.

GARDNER, H. 1978. *Developmental psychology.* Boston: Little, Brown.

GERRITZ, K. E. 1974. First graders' spelling of vowels: An exploratory study. Doctoral dissertation, Harvard Graduate School of Education.

GIBSON, E., AND LEVIN, H. 1975. *The psychology of reading.* Cambridge, Mass.: MIT Press.

GIBSON, W. 1969. *Persona: A style study for readers and writers.* New York: Random House.

GOODMAN, K. S. 1969. Analysis of oral reading miscues: applied psycholinguistics. *Reading Research Quarterly* 5:9-30.

GRAVES, D. H. 1975. An examination of the writing processes of seven year old children. *Research in the Teaching of English* 9:227-241.

————1978a. *Balance the basics: Let them write.* New York: Ford Foundation.

————1978b. *Let them write.* Speech presented at the Vermont Council on Reading meeting, North Clarendon, Vermont, May 1978.

————1979a. What children show us about revision. *Language Arts* 56:312-319.

————1979b. Let children show us how to help them write. University of New Hampshire (unpublished manuscript).

————1979c. The growth and development of first grade writers. Paper presented at the Canadian Council of Teachers of English Annual Meeting, Ottawa, Canada, May 1979.

HANNA, P. R., HODGES, R. E., AND HANNA, J. S. 1971. *Spelling: Structure and strategies.* Boston: Houghton Mifflin.

HARSTE, J., BURKE, C., AND WOODWARD, V. (forthcoming). Children's language and world: Initial encounters with print. In *Bridging the gap: Reader meets author,* ed. J. Langer and M. Smith-Burke. Newark, Del.: International Reading Association.

IRVING, K. J. 1975. Metalinguistic awareness and how it relates to the beginning reading process. Doctoral dissertation, Sarah Lawrence College.

JAKOBSON, R. 1968. *Child language, aphasia and phonological universals.* The Hague: Mouton.

KEGAN, R. G. 1977. Ego and truth: Personality and the Piaget Paradigm. Doctoral dissertation, Harvard University.

KELLOGG, R. 1969. *Analyzing children's art.* Palo Alto, Calif.: Mayfield.

KUHN, T. S. 1970. *The structure of scientific revolutions* (2nd ed.). Chicago: University of Chicago Press.

LARRICK, N. 1975. *A parent's guide to children's reading* (4th ed.). New York: Bantam Books.

LEFEVRE, C. A. 1973. A multidisciplinary approach to language and reading: some projections. In *The psycholinguistic nature of the reading process,* ed. K. S. Goodman. Detroit: Wayne State University Press.

MCDONALD, F. J. 1976. Beginning teacher evaluation study, phase II, 1973-74, executive summary report. Princeton, N.J.: Educational Testing Service (mimeo).

MARTIN, N. 1967. Stages of progress in language. In *Talking and writing,* ed. J. Britton. London: Methuen.

MOFFETT, J. 1968. *Teaching the universe of discourse.* Boston: Houghton Mifflin.

MOORHOUSE, A. C. 1953. *The triumph of the alphabet: A history of writing.* New York: Schuman.

OLDS, H. F. 1968. An experimental study of syntactical factors influencing children's comprehension. Doctoral dissertation, Harvard Graduate School of Education.

PROSPECT ARCHIVE AND CENTER FOR EDUCATION AND RESEARCH, North Bennington, Vermont. Archive of the child (unpublished documents).

READ, C. 1970. Children's perceptions of the sounds of English; phonology from three to six. Doctoral dissertation, Harvard University.

————1971. Pre-school children's knowledge of English phonology. *Harvard Educational Review* 41:1-34.

————1975. *Children's categorization of speech sounds in English.* Urbana, Ill.: National Council of Teachers of English.

ROE, A. 1952. *The making of a scientist.* New York: Dodd, Mead.

ROSEN, C., and ROSEN, H. 1973. *The language of primary school children.* Harmondsworth, England: Penguin Education.

RYAN, E. B. (forthcoming). Metalinguistic development and reading. In *The development of the reading process,* ed. F. Murray. Newark, Del.: International Reading Association.

SCHMANDT-BESSERAT, D. 1978. The earliest precursor of writing. *Scientific American* 238:50-59.

SMETHURST, W. 1975. *Teaching young children to read at home.* New York: McGraw-Hill.

SMITH, F. 1973. *Psycholinguistics and reading.* New York: Holt, Rinehart and Winston.

SÖDERBERGH, R. 1971. *Reading in early childhood.* Stockholm: Almqvist and Wiksell.

STEINBERG, D. D., AND STEINBERG, M. T. 1975. Reading before speaking. *Visible Language* 9:197-224.

TORREY, J. 1973. Learning to read without a teacher: A case study. In *Psycholinguistics and reading,* ed. F. Smith. New York: Holt, Rinehart and Winston.

ULLMAN, B. L. 1969. *Ancient writing and its influence.* Cambridge, Mass.: MIT Press. (Originally published in 1932.)

VENEZKY, R. L. 1970. *The structure of English orthography.* The Hague: Mouton.

VYGOTSKY, L. S. 1962. *Thought and language,* ed. and trans. E. Hanfman and G. Vakar. Cambridge, Mass.: MIT Press. (Originally published in 1934.)

WEBER, R. 1970. First-graders' use of grammatical context in reading. In *Basic studies on reading,* ed. H. Levin and J. P. Williams. New York: Basic Books.

WEIR, R. H., AND VENEZKY, R. 1973. Spelling-to-sound patterns. In *The psycholinguistic nature of the reading process,* ed. K. S. Goodman. Detroit: Wayne State University Press.

WERNER, H. 1948. *Comparative psychology of mental development.* New York: Science Editions.

WERNER, H., AND KAPLAN, B. 1963. *Symbol formation.* New York: Wiley.

WHITE, R. W. 1952. *Lives in progress.* New York: Dryden Press.

WOLF, T. 1977. Reading reconsidered. *Harvard Educational Review* 47:411-429.

Index